EVIL RISING

Fred DeRuvo

Evil Rising

Copyright © 2011 by Study-Grow-Know

All rights reserved. Written permission must be secured from the publisher to use or reproduce any part of this book, except brief quotations in critical reviews or articles.

Published in Scotts Valley, California, by Study-Grow-Know
www.studygrowknow.com • www.adroitpublications.com

Scripture quotations, unless otherwise noted, are from The Holy Bible, King James Version. This version is in the public domain.

Images used in this publication (unless otherwise noted) are from clipartconnection.com and used with permission, ©2007 JUPITERIMAGES, and its licensors. All rights reserved.

Any Woodcuts used herein are in the Public Domain and free of copyright.

All Figure illustrations used in this book were created by the author and protected under copyright laws, © 2010, unless otherwise noted.

Cover Design and Interior Layout: Fred DeRuvo

Edited by: Hannah Richards

Library of Congress Cataloging-in-Publication Data

DeRuvo, Fred, 1957 –

ISBN 0977424421
EAN-13 978-0977424429

1. Religion – Demonology & Satanism

Evil Rising

CONTENTS

Foreword:		5
Chapter 1:	The Coming Planned Chaos	7
Chapter 2:	God Reigns	11
Chapter 3:	For There Shall Be Great Distress	15
Chapter 4:	The Black Awakening	22
Chapter 5:	As It Was in the Days of Egypt	30
Chapter 6:	Aliens, Demons, and Hybrids	39
Chapter 7:	One-World Government	46
Chapter 8:	One-World Religion	53
Chapter 9:	Hell Hath Fury	60
Chapter 10:	Trans-humanism & Synthetics	71
Chapter 11:	The Illuminati	91
Chapter 12:	Absolute Obscenity	100
Chapter 13:	Back to Egypt	110
Chapter 14:	Superstorms!	116
Chapter 15:	Muslim Sends the Wrong Message	122
Chapter 16:	The Danger of Leaving Islam Unchecked	128
Chapter 17:	Inside Islam	139
Chapter 18:	Satan on the Rise	158
Epilogue		170

"for this cause God shall send them strong delusion, that they should believe a lie: That they all might be damned who believed not the truth, but had pleasure in unrighteousness..." (2 Thessalonians 2:11-12 KJV)

The author would like to extend major thanks to *Marie Swanson* for all the information she gathered from a variety of sources for use in this book. Without her help, this endeavor would have been much more difficult. Thank you, Marie, for your dedication to the Lord and to see His purposes come to fruition.

FOREWORD

Anyone with even a modicum of intelligence can see what is happening in the world today. While there are differing opinions as to *why* the world is in the shape it is in, and *where* this world is heading, the truth remains that something evil is on the rise.

For the last few decades, evil seems to have ramped up not only its presence, but its work throughout the globe. What used to be hidden has now become much more mainstream. It is as if evil couldn't care less that it is seen. It is not that evil has become reckless. It has become *emboldened* to do what evil does best; *destroy*.

In many ways, this book reads like a science fiction novel. There are things in here that the reader will find very difficult to believe. In fact, let it be known from the outset that as the author, I have difficulties believing some of the very things I discuss in this book.

The reality that needs to be considered is not whether all of these things are true or not. What matters is that there are a growing number of individuals throughout the world that *do* believe these things and do so without equivocation.

Believing in something does not make it true. People believe in all sorts of things, and the belief itself does not mean that the object of that belief is fact. It simply means that particular individual guides his or her own life based on that specific belief-system. This is true of all people and all beliefs, including atheists and agnostics. Someone can be thoroughly convinced that there is no God of any sort at all. Because of that, they will live their life according to how they believe. It simply makes sense.

In this book, there are many things that may be new to the reader. The first reaction may be to state, "that is crazy." It may well be true that at least some of what is discussed herein *is crazy*, but again, that does not stop people from exercising their faith in it. Because they believe it, they adjust their lives to fit it.

I would caution the reader about simply casting these things off as the rantings and/or ramblings of those who are on the edge of sanity, or those who have crossed over from sanity to insanity. It is too easy to do that. What is more important is attempting to determine *why* people believe the things they believe and understanding the impact it has on those lives.

The things that people believe not only impact their own lives, but society at large, to some degree. The stronger the belief, the greater the impact.

Is all of this part of a plan to deceive society? I believe it is, and this book is meant to expose a number of the deceptions that are currently being used to accomplish this goal.

However, we must always understand that it is God who – above all things – works everything out according to the purposes of His own will. He leaves nothing to chance, and all things are allowed or done according to His plan.

With this in mind, we must ask ourselves: why the deception? What is being planned for global society that God allows, that will have a major impact on the lives of the people of this planet?

Delusions and deceptions come with a heavy price. Those who succumb to it will risk losing their eternal souls to the kingdom of darkness. Those who – by God's strength, grace, and insight – overcome these delusions, gain access to God's Kingdom of eternal light and truth.

Fred DeRuvo, March 2011

1

The Coming Planned Chaos

What would you do if the person you were working alongside and had known for a number of years without warning turned into a cold-blooded, emotionless killer? If with no pretense or prior warning, this human being with whom you had been carrying on a conversation pulled out a gun or a knife and attacked you for no apparent reason?

How do you believe you would react to that type of assault? What if in an instant, people like your co-worker, who were friendly one moment, then cold and zombie-like the next, all turned into something like killers, acting more like robots than people?

Yes, it sounds like something out of a Sci-Fi/Thriller movie. As if on cue, thousands of seemingly normal human beings become assassins in the time it takes to think one thought. Unbelievable, you say? Difficult to imagine? Impossible that something like this could occur?

Think again. What may be unbelievable to the average mind is not at all unbelievable to the genius psychopaths who may be lurking behind the reality that we see in our daily lives. These hidden leaders have worked toward, and longed for, the day when peace would become chaos. They have dedicated themselves to overturning this current world order, replacing it with a new one; a world order where the world is literally one.

These individuals who resolutely remain in the deep shadows, enjoying their anonymity, have worked under the cloak of evil darkness to bring about a day in which one man will rule the world. They dream and plan for a day when they will worship the physical representation of their master, Satan, in the form of Antichrist.

These individuals have perfected the art of mind-control, subversion, and government policies in order that their purposes will come to fruition. They allow nothing to stop them, nothing to trip them up, and they have worked from one generation to the next, shifting society toward their desired end.

The coming cataclysmic chaos that may well be planned to occur will seem to the average person to be an accident. It will appear to be something beyond the control of the greatest minds. This coming chaos will be so perfect and evil that though it will make the world seem out of control, it will be perfectly controlled by those who hold the strings deep in the shadows. The purpose of this coming chaos is to destroy the hopes and dreams of the world's societies. It is to rip from the average person any sense of tranquility, peace, confidence, and well-being.

The coming chaos must be of a level that will cause people to die due to the fear of what may be the result. While this planned global turmoil will be the worst this world has ever seen, it will not destroy everything. It will only destroy enough so that people will willingly give up their freedoms, their dreams, and their rights in exchange for the promise of peace, safety, and security.

Think of it. Life goes on as it has from the beginning, and though it has its ups and downs, you have no reason to believe that the economy will not bounce back. You believe these economic bumps in the road are just that, bumps that will smooth out.

Yet things continue to grow worse. The promised economic upturn never really arrives. The policies of our government continue to move in a direction that seems to take away liberties from citizens, while granting privileges to those not here legally.

Though the president tries to reassure America that things will turn around, that he is in this for the long haul, his words sound and seem empty to you because of his own actions. While he promises one thing, our president seems intent on doing other things that are all too often the opposite of what he promises.

Yet the president seems to be undeterred by his own shallowness and transparency, acting as if his promises are being fulfilled when everyone except the most blind can see that they are *not* being fulfilled. In spite of growing criticism of our president and his administration's policies toward Muslims and Islam, he continues unmoved, dutifully ignoring the will of the people of this land. He smiles in our face as he picks our pockets. He harbors and befriends those who hate America and have promised to destroy it. He does whatever he chooses to do and even the media seems in on it, unwilling to report on the administration's alleged illegal activities.

One day, the bottom falls out. The very land where you have lived all your life, and your parents before you, and their parents before them, has somehow gone bankrupt. America can no longer support its own massive debt, nor can it support its many programs and policies that have been instituted under various administrations.

America – land of the free, home of the brave – is in the throes of death, and you are witnessing it! This uncertainty has left you numb with fear. This fear has spread across the nation and across the world as you watch TV in horror, seeing one country after another collapse under its own weight.

You see the violence begin and build to a crescendo, as you have never seen before. You see the looting by people who can no longer afford to buy anything because the banks have closed or gone bankrupt themselves. These are frightening times indeed, as it appears as though every man is against his neighbor and a brother against his sister and a sister against her mother.

What will you do? Where will you go? Whom can you trust? You reach for your Bible, wishing with all your heart that you had taken the time to study it, memorize it, and use it in your prayers to God. Your heart's desire now is to humble yourself before God, asking Him to save you from a world that has exploded. You submit to Him – *finally* – confessing your sin, receiving His forgiveness, and endeavoring to live *for* Him with however many days or hours remain.

Outside your home or office, the sound of violence draws near. People have gone crazy. On the TV, you see people shooting each other, shooting at helicopters attempting to film the scenes. You see police officers turning on average citizens and some of them even turning on fellow officers. What is happening? When will it end? Where is God?

2

God Reigns

God is the same place He has always been: on His throne, ruling all things, allowing all things that occur, and by them, glorifying Himself. God is near and He receives your humble submission to Him gladly.

He is your protector, your advocate, your Lord and God. Nothing will happen to you unless it goes past Him first. He has your life in His hand and you finally realize it! You finally come to that point where you understand what it means to be a living authentic Christian, one who has given himself over to God for His purposes, not yours.

I do not believe we are aware of just how dark the world is to become as we move closer to the edge of the precipice we know as The

Tribulation period. The reality of this growing darkness (something Russ Dizdar calls "The Black Awakening") already seems palpable.

We read God's Word, we study its meaning, we see what life on this planet has become, yet we seem unable to process the full magnitude of this coming blackness. Think of the fact that if we are moving to a time when God will pour out His wrath on the world for seven years, it will not all of a sudden be smooth sailing one day and then terrible confusion and chaos the next, like turning on or off a light switch.

In order for this world to become so drastically malevolent, it will have to happen in stages and over a long period of time, but it will progress toward the intended goal. The reality of this coming situation – once I began to seriously consider it – made me aware of the horrors that this generation is moving toward.

I fully believe that we are moving to a period when Satan will push for God's overthrow in an attempt his very soul depends upon winning. If that is the case, then we must consider the fact that this will be all out war, moving out in two directions:

1. *Satan's controlled anger and hatred for God will be deployed against those who are His, and*
2. *Satan will gather every ounce of his strength, intelligence, and resources to overcome all obstacles and use those of this world (who do not belong to God) as his pawns in his own epic struggle against God*

Authentic Christians must stop and consider the ramifications of this coming darkness. Even though we know that Satan is already defeated now because of the cross, the only route he can take is the route preordained by God. Satan has no choice but to proceed on the path to attempt to usurp God for the last time.

Jesus told us that no sooner would the Church be born than Satan would secretly infiltrate the visible Church with his own agents (cf.

Matthew 13:24-30). Notice the enemy comes when the master of the house is sleeping. In other words, the enemy sows seeds of tares under the cover of darkness, when he is less likely to be seen. We can read about the numerous attempts of Satan to destroy the church from within and without in the book of Acts, which highlights the first thirty years of the Church.

Since the birth of the Church, Satan has been busy infiltrating the visible Church with *error, laziness*, a *lack of maturity* and *spirituality*, and a complete lack of *familiarity with God's Word*. He has done this by placing key people in key positions of authority. He has also done this by placing in the visible Church those who appear to be average people, who teach Sunday school classes, act as Deacons or even Elders, and at times even act as pastors. At the same time, outside of the visible Church, he has been busy cultivating a worldview among the average person that glorifies self to the point of deification. Satan has been preparing for God's overthrow since *before* the Garden of Eden, when he fell through his own pride. He is serious and refuses to back down in spite of the fact that he will be physically overthrown in the end, as he was spiritually overthrown at Calvary.

Satan is playing for keeps. He is real, as are his goals. The Lord God is *allowing* Satan to play himself out, and the people of this planet are the battlefield. What we need to become desperately aware of is the amount of loathing and hatred that drives Satan. We need to understand the loathing that he carries deep within him has created an unstoppable drive to *conquer*. We know what the outcome for him and those who follow him will be. However, we must understand that if we are the generation that Jesus spoke of in the Olivet Discourse (cf. Matthew 24, Mark 13, Luke 21), then hell will be emptied to wreak chaos and havoc on this earth during the time period known as the Tribulation.

This has been happening in incremental stages. As the spiritual tsunami builds, it will finally come to a point of no return – and more than that, will overtake all civilization as we know it. Friends, if these are in fact those days, then we can be assured of the fact that as the darkness approaches, life will become very dark indeed. We cannot walk around with our head in the clouds. We must be prepared for the possibility of danger, just as the first century apostles and disciples of Jesus lived in that constant shadow.

I hope you will read this book with an open mind and an open Bible. I pray that the Lord will grant us a greater awareness of what He is doing, even as Satan gears up for his final challenge, which will ultimately end in abject defeat. He knows that he is already overcome and that only serves to bring out that much more hatred.

As the darkness enters, we must realize that while God is our Savior, our Lord, and certainly our protector, He does not want His children to be stupid. He expects us to be as wise as serpents and as gentle as doves.

I believe the time is rapidly approaching when the light is going to become very dim, very dim indeed, though we know that God will never leave or forsake us and nothing can separate us from His love (cf. Romans 8). We must throw ourselves on Him daily, moment by moment, with the intent to walk through the darkness by faith in Him for as long as we are meant to be here on this planet.

I pray that this book will open blind eyes and root out the spiritual immaturity found within so many Christians today. The enemy is on the prowl and he plays for keeps. By God's leave, Satan is going to make life a hell on earth. How are you going to react? How will you be and remain strong in Christ?

The coming days are not for the frail or spiritually immature. The coming days are for those who walk by faith, trusting in the One who lives within us. May God be glorified in and through us as this planet moves steadily and quickly toward the approaching darkness.

3

For There Shall Be Great Distress...

It is safe to say that the visible Church is most likely *not* prepared for just how bad things will get as the time approaches for the coming cataclysmic chaos. We spend our time debating theology, becoming angry at other Christians who oppose our views. We try to determine who is right, who is wrong, and who is deceived.

The reality is that while we are embroiled in this type of wasted effort and energy, Satan clearly gains an advantage because Christians are preoccupied with *peripheral* matters, as opposed to our primary purpose, which is *evangelizing* the lost. How could this be? How could we as Christians come to a point of being so preoccupied with debate of doctrine that we seem unable to see those who are in desperate need of salvation?

Both Paul and Peter (as well as Jesus in His Olivet Discourse) explain to us in no uncertain terms *what* these end times will become and the effect these times will have on those who live during them. We read about this period of time in John's first epistle as well.

So what is this great distress that Jesus speaks of that will take place on this earth as the end approaches? This author believes that it is a spiritual darkness that will envelop this planet and will be unlike any darkness that has ever been perpetrated on this world. It will manifest itself in many ways, but primarily in *deception*, false miracles, and signs and wonders.

Paul is very clear about the strength of this deception. He states in his letter to the Thessalonians that the delusion itself will be exceedingly strong. He warns, *"for this cause God shall send them strong delusion, that they should believe a lie: That they all might be damned who believed not the truth, but had pleasure in unrighteousness"* (2 Thessalonians 2:11-12).

In these two verses, Paul tells us *what* and he tells us *why*. The "what" refers to the deception itself. Please note that it is God Himself who actually sends the delusion. How does He do it and in what form will it appear? That's what this book is about. Why God does it is found in the last sentence. It is ultimately so that the people who buy into *the* lie will understand the reason for their damnation. In other words, they will be thoroughly without any excuse whatsoever.

Some may ask, *"How can God – who is said to be loving – purposefully send a delusion that causes people to buy the lie that ultimately sends them to hell for all eternity?"* It must be remembered that God sends the lie because it is clear to Him that the people who end up believing it preferred to *"[have] pleasure in unrighteousness."* God does nothing arbitrarily. He has a purpose for everything that happens. Beyond this, He provides everyone with every possible chance they could have to turn to Him, receiving *His* truth, which is the only truth.

Those who reject it repeatedly are to blame for their own ultimate failure to make the correct decision, which meant embracing the truth. Instead, they deliberately embraced the lie. As such, they are not simply rejecting absolute truth, but they are also rejecting God Himself since He is Truth. Because they reject Him, He is perfectly justified in rejecting them. That is how it works, and God is not in the least responsible for the decisions we make here since we have the ability to make a decision either for or against Him.

While God wants no one to perish, He did not create automatons. He created people with the ability to think and reason, and that sets us apart from the animals, which live largely by *instinct*. Theirs is an act/react way of life. Human beings, on the other hand, make millions of decisions each day based on thought and reason.

The first verse quoted from 2 Thessalonians 2 starts out with "*for this cause.*" The question must be asked: for *what* cause? What is the reason that God sends the delusion that causes people to believe the lie? In the previous verses, Paul explains that the "day of the Lord" could not have occurred yet because a number of things must happen first.

In verse 3, Paul refers to a great falling away (or apostasy) that must ripple throughout the entire world. This falling away references leaving sound doctrine to follow that which simply tickles the ears. This author personally believes that this situation has been occurring for quite some time, but within the last ten to fifteen years has become far more noticeable. Many within established churches are leaving those churches to find ones that are more to their liking. Either that or the church they are associated with moves off track and becomes something else entirely.

The name of the game today is to keep the people in the pews satisfied so that they will return every week, opening their wallets each time. It does not do to have people leave one church to find another because of the truth that is being preached at the one church. Let's change things up so that people come to church because they know they will be entertained. Moreover, they will not have to deal with those pesky theologies and doctrines that cause them to discern their own quality of life before God.

Too many preachers today want their people to be happy. If the topic of sin is discussed (except as a joke), the guilt many feel from hearing about it will drive people away. They will simply find another church that does not try to make them look inward. They will find a church that *entertains* them.

Rather than allowing that to happen, many churches have given themselves a spiritual *makeover*. They have become more modern, more upbeat, and more celebratory. They discuss the "good" things about God such as His love, His mercy, His tenderness, and His patience. They dutifully avoid discussing His holiness, His hatred of sin, His deep sense of justice, and His ultimate punishment of evildoers.

What this means is that the people who stay with a church that changes into the Hollywood version of Christianity, or those who leave a doctrinally solid church to find greener pastures elsewhere, are already being deceived. They are being deceived because they do not want to acknowledge the entire character of God, preferring instead to simply discuss the pleasurable aspects of His character and personality.

Because they have made the decision to segregate God's attributes, they obviously are not interested in the fullness of His personality. They want to hear only those things that make them comfortable and so they begin to deceive themselves.

The enemy of our souls comes in and personifies that deception, normally by directing those people to a church where only a partial gospel is taught. A partial gospel is worse than no gospel at all because pastors and teachers, who wind up itching people's ears with their half-truths and outright lies, are introducing a person to something that does not exist in the Bible anywhere. However, because of their position of authority, people believe them. They take their teachings to heart and become even further deceived.

In essence, then, the delusion that God sends is simply a reaction to the fact that people like the ones described above do not want to hear the truth at all. They *prefer* the lie because the lie makes them feel worthwhile. The lie places no responsibility on them at all. It frees them from having to agree and cooperate with God as He seeks to create within us His holy character. This author believes that this falling away or apostasy that Paul speaks of is in full swing now.

The other thing Paul explains is that once this falling away or apostasy becomes full-fledged, it will naturally lead up to the unveiling of *the* man of sin. Here, Paul is obviously referring to a specific individual. Though the *spirit* of Antichrist has been in the world forever, it will culminate in one specific person at the end of this age who will be the world's final dictator.

Paul tells us what this man will be like. The fact that Paul refers to him as the "man of sin" speaks volumes (v. 3). This man of sin or son of perdition will do two main things:

1. Oppose everything that connects with God, and
2. Exalt himself

This guy will be so evil that he will think of himself as God. He will oppose everything and everyone who worships the true God because he will want to be worshipped. He will not want to share his own perceived glory with anyone else, and his life will be noted for the two tracks of attempting to defeat all that endeavors to attack him either directly or indirectly, and constantly lifting himself up higher than anything so that all will worship him. That is his twofold purpose.

Those who have bought into the lie will do so because they will first reject the truth. They reject the truth because it makes them uncomfortable. They search until they find something that they can embrace, which is untruth or the lie.

Since they have already decided that they do not want the truth, God will send a very strong delusion that allows them to embrace the lie with everything that is within them. When they see the Antichrist on the world's stage, embracing him will be exceedingly easy because of the accompanying signs and wonders that he is able to accomplish. People will be astounded and will see him as being so charismatic, loving, and intelligent that they will be unable to keep from being swept up into throng of people who are tripping over themselves to be the first in line to worship this man.

Once people give themselves over to the Antichrist, God will continue to give them opportunities to reject the lie and receive the truth. This will continue until the time that the Mark of the Beast is given and made mandatory. Without it, people will not be able to buy or sell (cf. Revelation 13:17). This will be the final option. Those who submit to receiving the mark will be forever lost. Those who opt to not take the mark will have more chances to be saved. Understand that only those who refuse to take the mark will understand that by taking the mark, they will literally be trading their souls to the devil. It will take that type of understanding to refuse to accept the mark because of the ramifications of not taking it.

The lie is at work in this world now. This lie is causing people both great and small to move further and further away from God, rejecting His truth for all that is not true. As the lie continues to work itself through society as yeast works through the dough, those who embrace the lie will find it more difficult to find their way to God, while at the same time, they will find it increasingly easier to embrace the lie because of the delusion that God sends.

This is the beginning of the great distress that is going to come to this planet and is, to some degree, already here. As the reader goes further through this book, the various ways in which this same lie will be made manifest will be clearly seen.

4

The Black Awakening

Russ Dizdar has written a book called *The Black Awakening* (BA). In it, he discusses some extremely incredible things that he believes are occurring within the spiritual realm and which have spilled over into this physical realm with greater clarity and increasing menace. The things that Dizdar discusses are difficult for the average person to believe. If we were to simply look at Dizdar's book, and the things he says have occurred in his life, in a vacuum, it would be very difficult if not impossible to believe them. However, we do not need to look at Dizdar's book in a vacuum. We can look throughout society and determine truthfulness based on what we see from a variety of areas. Again, this does not mean that what Dizdar and others say they have experienced is true. It means that there is a greater degree of validity because of the fact that we are not left to solely rely on Dizdar as our means of verifying authenticity.

Dizdar is a pastor and has had years of experience dealing with the spiritual. He states he has dealt with demon-possessed people, those from Satanist cults and covens as well as those individuals he calls *Satanic Super Soldiers*.[1] These "super soldiers" are simply and for the most part in *wait* mode until they are released onto the world to carry out their preprogrammed missions.

If we find this difficult to believe, then we need merely to look back in history to the SS Nazi. The average Nazi was brainwashed into thinking a number of things that, for them, *became* truth:

1. The Jews were *the* problem in the world and needed to be dealt with, and
2. Germans were told that unless they did something to protect the Aryan race, it would disappear

Hitler was raised up by Satan to accomplish his goal, that of eradicating Jews from the face of this world. People involved in Hitler's "Final Solution" fully believed that what they were doing was right. After all, it was war, and all is fair in love and war. Since they had been brainwashed by someone who carried with himself such charisma, Hitler became someone who was difficult to ignore.

Germans fell in love with the man because of his high ideals and his goals for the German people. For the rest of the world, the name Hitler came to stand for anti-Semitism on a grand scale. Hitler was evil incarnate, and in some ways was likely a test that allowed Satan to

---

[1] http://www.peeringintodarkness.com/?p=1183

see what he could achieve through one individual. Hitler was the test subject in order for Satan to refine and hone his skills for the coming man of sin that Paul speaks of in 2 Thessalonians 2. Satan would learn through his empowering of Hitler what would and would not work. These notes he would keep waiting for the future opportunity to fully incarnate his own "son," the Antichrist himself.

Nazi men and women fully believed that they were the superior race and that all Jews certainly, along with anyone who was considered to be defective, must be eradicated. By doing so, not only would the entire remaining human race be "cleaned up," but the Aryan race especially would no longer be in danger of disappearing or becoming impure due to potential cross-breeding of German with Jew.

If we consider our world today, anti-Semitism has once again grown at an alarming rate. Leading the pack of hatred toward Jewish people is Islam, which creates radical Muslim children who are taught from birth that Jews are pigs and apes and certainly not worthy of continuing to live. Like the Nazis of decades ago, today's radical Muslim believes that it is the Jew that has created all the ills in society, and because of that, must be eradicated.

We have heard the ramblings and rhetoric of the Iranian President Ahmadinejad, who has without equivocation condemned the Jew and will not rest until every last Jew is removed from the Middle East. Except for comments in protest here and there, the world looks the other way.

As we delve more deeply into the meaning of the Black Awakening, we learn that those involved in it will one day rise to create a kingdom of darkness that will engulf the entire world. This is the central core belief for those who look to the Black Awakening that will one day spill out across this globe.

"One of the most persistent rumors involves the legend of Karl the Great (of the Holy Roman Empire of German Nation), known in the west as Charles the Great or Charlemagne. Though physically buried in the German village of Aachen, it is believed that the "astral form" of this emperor sleeps in the mysterious depths of a subterranean throne room, surrounded by his strongest knights, gnomes, frost giants and fire giants, Valkyries and other "Volk," awaiting the final liberation of his country and kinsmen; that he will rule over a thousand year kingdom of Aryan dominion. Other accounts maintain this entity is the spirit of the emperor Frederich Barbarossa.

"Within the ancient "mythologies" of the "Ice People," are the prophecies that at a future point in time, though time itself is a variable, the "Watcher-god" Heimdall will sound his trumpet to summon the children of Loki. This semi-divine/human Sixth Race will break their bonds and unite with the forces of chaos to sail from the land of the Niflheim, located in an astral plane beyond the auroras, waging the final battle with the current "usurpers" of the planet to culminate in the enthronement of their vaticinated king. It is this anticipated kingdom and its preparation that has been the goal of the ancient spirits. This is the heart of the Black Awakening. And it is the understanding of the "Volk" that clarifies this motivation and interprets the history of the human race."[2]

Ultimately, the Black Awakening is that coming kingdom which will allow the dark lord to take the throne, ruling the world and dictating to all of his subjects. How will this occur? Those Satanic Super Soldiers currently in society will one day *wake* to their true reason for being. They will fulfill their missions throughout the various parts of the world for which they have been programmed.

Dizdar explains that these Satanic Super Soldiers are such because of years of mind-control techniques and Satanic Ritual Abuse, which

---

[2] http://peeringintodarkness.com/?p=1292

has created individuals with multiple personality disorder (MPD). Often these individuals are not even aware of what is hidden deep within them, until such a time as they are called on to perform their duties. These people are also often referred to as *cult multiples* because it has been through their association with the occult that their many personalities have been developed. Often, this begins at early childhood. Dizdar states that the term *Black Awakening* "*is a term that many of the 'cult multiples... satanic chosen ones use to describe a time when they will be activated to unleash chaos and anarchy into the USA and other countries...to cause collapse and pave the way for a 'new world order' and the rise of the antichrist.*

"*There are over 4 million diagnosed cases of MPD/SRA......and 4+million more who are still out there. Someone has orchestrated this. There is a vast underground at work.*

"*These satanic super soldiers as I call them are placed everywhere as sleepers waiting for the call. The secret power of lawlessness...and the great 'rebellion'(chaos-anarchy-coo) spoken about in 2 Thessalonians is directly connected to this event.*"[3]

Dizdar, who believes in the coming Black Awakening, defines it as: "*The [Black Awakening] BA will be carried out by the hundreds of thousands of highly trained...programmed and demonized 'satanic chosen ones', who will be activated from their 'sleeper' status and released to carry out their pre-chosen tasks.*

"*The BA will occur as the spiritual air is turning darker...it will happen when antichrist and his regime is ready to come to power. They must collapse the current powers that be so they can replace them.*"[4]

For those who have done any research at all on mind-control techniques, the terms MK-Ultra and Project Monarch are known. Wheth-

---

[3] http://www.whale.to/b/dizdar.html
[4] Ibid

er or not MK-Ultra, Project Monarch, and other events actually exist is not something this book will delve into. Again, what matters is that there are people who fully believe that these techniques and projects did or do exist and they believe the results of these programs are seen in the Satanic Super Soldiers. Dizdar also refers to these individuals as the Chosen Ones because they were specifically chosen to become a soldier in the coming holocaust that is designed to recreate the world, giving birth to a new one-world government that the elite will rule, subjugating the rest of the population that is not part of the elite or its structure.

While the author realizes that much of this sounds like something from a science fiction novel or movie, the reason for that is obvious, or should be. What better way to desensitize the masses to the plan of the elite but by revealing that plan way ahead of time through the venue of science fiction? Science fiction proper dates back to 1926 with Hugo Gemsback using the term *scientifiction* in his publication of that time. A few years later, the term was changed to *science fiction*. However, most are familiar with the works of Jules Verne and others who wrote about fantastic ships and adventures that were clearly science fiction. His works such as *20,000 Thousand Leagues Under the Sea*, *A Journey to the Center of the Earth*, and *Around the World in Eighty Days* all testify of his use of science fiction. These works were published from 1864 to 1873.

Since that time, the field of science fiction has expanded to include television and movies. Shows like *Star Trek*, *My Favorite Martian*, and even *The Wild, Wild, West* either offered looks into the future, or introduced viewers to science fiction tools and theories. Movies such as *Forbidden Planet, 2001: A Space Odyssey* and many more too numerous to count all played a very important role in desensitizing humanity to the entire area of science fiction.

Society has become used to it, and in fact believes strongly that many of the gadgets and ideas used or discussed in these TV shows, novels, and movies could actually exist. However, there will always be a segment of society that does not believe it, and for them any thought or discussion of the possible reality of those things within the science fiction genre is either wishful or illogical thinking.

It is interesting how Satan has used his lie to be what it needs to be for all people. For those who would never believe in the possibility of science fiction, they are desensitized. For those who find the subject fascinating and possible, they are given greater glimpses into that world.

If you were to ask the average person about the possibility of much of the science fiction genre actually being real, they would either laugh at you, or state without equivocation that those things are only possible in the special effects industry of Hollywood. Yet, there is a growing number of people who not only believe in some of the possibilities that have been portrayed on the silver screen and elsewhere, but fully believe that humanity is not only capable of it, but has in fact created a good deal of it.

Many of these people are simply shrugged off as loons, or those who are deeply entrenched in conspiracy theories. They are believed to be slightly or majorly off in the head, not to be taken seriously. They are also not anyone to be concerned about because they are generally seen as harmless.

So it is when we delve into the subject of the Black Awakening, Satanic Super Soldiers, and the Chosen Ones; reactions will vary depending upon the group that learns of them. Are these individuals who are said will one day wake up and perform their mission *real*? Again, it is impossible to know.

Dizdar speaks of these soldiers as though they do exist. He also explains what they are capable of doing. *"They are made to do things like...keep tabs on a person...perform a ritual...sex...harm...kill... Any-*

thing they want done under that form of mind control can be done."[5] Dizdar also notes that many of these personalities are highly trained killers and have shown no remorse at all for their killings...*if* they even remember doing them. While these Satanic Super Soldiers are not doing what they are preprogrammed to do, they are considered to be *sleepers*. At the appointed time, they will awake and the inner personality that has been trained under mind-control will take over and do the job for which it has been prepared.

Dizdar also refers to the beings *behind* these people as Extra-Dimensional Beings, or EDBs. Many believe that they are aliens or ETs; however, it seems clear because of their belief-systems that they are much more in line with demons simply masquerading as aliens, or extra-dimensional beings. We will delve into this in later chapters.[6]

Regarding the Super Soldier, many TV series and movies have been produced on this same subject. These super soldiers are seen to be part human, part cyborg, with heightened awareness and superior abilities and powers. Again, it appears as though Hollywood is giving us the plan in a way that only allows us to think in terms of science fiction, not reality. When we step away from it and think logically about all of the potential and known cover-ups within our government and other governments, it becomes more plausible to realize that at least some of this could exist right under our noses.

---

[5] http://www.whale.to/b/dizdar.html
[6] For more information on this subject, please see two books by the author, *Demons in Disguise* and *Nephilim Nightmare*.

5

As It Was in the Days of Egypt

The ancient civilization of Egypt was known for many things. We immediately think of the Sphinx, the pyramids, the seemingly impossible things that the Egyptians managed to do – and yet they were thousands of years behind modern times! That does not seem to matter since no one has been able to figure out how the pyramids were built, for instance. The mystery surrounding these monolithic masterpieces remains just that, a mystery.

How were the pyramids built? How did they accomplish what they accomplished with the ancient tools they possessed, ancient thinking, and without cranes, jackhammers, and other modern conveniences?

At this point in history, it is impossible to know for sure; though one thing may help us to understand just how they gained the knowledge they gained.

Some say Ancient Egypt had its beginnings around 5,500 B.C., until about 30 B.C., when Egypt became a province of the Roman Empire. There were certainly some very high points for Egypt during this long period of time.

It was during the time of the Old Kingdom that Egypt enjoyed much of its success in areas of technology, agriculture, and other areas as well. This was during the third millennium B.C.

Within the Old Kingdom, the Fourth Dynasty is considered to be the Golden Age due to the building of three additional pyramids, as well as the Sphinx. If we look at the possible time of Noah, we are looking at a period of time during the third millennium B.C. as well.

We know that the world was destroyed (if the Bible is taken to be true) because of the fact that humanity was so evil that all people ever thought about was evil (cf. Genesis 6:5). It is just verses before God sees that everything on the earth except Noah was evil that we are introduced to the Nephilim. Many believe that these Nephilim were the offspring of fallen angels and human women.

Whether this is true or not, we *do* know that by the time of Adam and Eve, Satan and his fallen angels already existed because they had already fallen through rebellion and disobedience to God. Once Satan was able to cause Eve and ultimately Adam to sin, Satan gained access to the earth. Not only that, but in essence, he gained the title deed to the earth, something which Jesus regained upon His death, burial, and resurrection (cf. Revelation 5).

Since Satan and the fallen angels now had access to the earth, they also had access to people. Some believe – and this author concurs – that since this situation existed prior to Noah's time, it is not only possible, but likely, that Satan and his minions were busy teaching groups who were open to them the mysteries of the occult. It is believed that this is at least one of the reasons why Ancient Egypt had become so technologically savvy.

It is clear from the writings of the Ancient Egyptians that they were occultic in nature. They worshipped many deities (including Pharaoh), believed that the afterlife was something that was measured by the works done in this life, and through their understanding of the occult (or secret wisdom), they were able to do what other civilizations could not do.

After the Flood, all of these civilizations would have been wiped out, including the Nephilim. However, the fallen angels as well as Satan continued to exist. Why could they not have spent thousands of years teaching new groups this same type of secret occult widsom? This author believes that is exactly what has happened.

This is seen in the Third Reich and Hitler's desire to learn everything he could learn about the occult. He believed that it was through the occult he came to gain the power he had to mesmerize the German people. This then allowed him to call forth the powers of hell in his attempt to eradicate Jews and rule the world.

It is interesting that Hitler, who was very likely empowered, to some degree at least, by Satan, believed that he needed to destroy all Jews. This anti-Semitism is one of the hallmarks of occult thought. The reason for this is simple enough. We know that Jesus in His humanity is Jewish, having come from the Tribe of Judah (cf. Revelation 5). We also know that salvation comes from Jesus alone.

Though Jesus has already lived His human life and completely fulfilled God the Father's every command, Satan continues to hate the Jews because it is through them that salvation came to the world. The other very important reason has to do with the fact that at every turn, Satan wants to bring God's plans to naught. If he can accomplish that, then he will be able to prove that not only is God a liar, but that he – Satan – is more powerful than God Himself. If he ever arrived at this point, then he will fulfill his own desires to make himself greater than God.

Satan wants more than anything to kill every Jew from the face of this earth so that there will be no Jews left to inherit the Kingdom of God during the Millennial Reign of Jesus. If Satan can accomplish this, then God's promises to restore Jews (the Remnant) to the Promised Land will never be fulfilled. If this happens, Satan will have won.

Of course, it only takes a cursory look at Satan's attempts to know that he has been thwarted at every turn. If we can base the future on the past, we know that Satan will not succeed. Yet he tries, and that is all he really has – his *attempts*.

Just as he did in times past, Satan has worked very hard to overthrow God's purposes *before* they happen. He began with his plans for humanity in the Garden of Eden. He thought if he could cause Adam and Eve to fall, it would destroy God's plans. It didn't because God's plans went much further than simply the Creation.

In Genesis chapter three, God issues the punishment for the fall to Adam and Eve and also to Satan for the role he played in the situation. During God's sentencing, He stated that the woman's seed would crush Satan's seed. Satan is not an idiot, and immediately he understood that God spoke of a Messiah who would ultimately destroy him (Satan). This seed would come from the woman. Please note that in chapter three, when God says this, He does not allude to Adam or another man. He simply says "her seed" (cf. Genesis 3:15). This is likely an allusion to the virgin birth. Be that as it may, it became clear to Satan that he needed to destroy a first son that Adam and Eve had. Satan worked within Cain to kill Abel, thereby destroying *both* sons; one who became a murderer and the other the murdered.

Eve continued to have more children and Seth became the next son that we learn about. What quickly became apparent to Satan was that the Messiah was not to be born yet. As he watched the sons and daughters of Adam and Eve flourish and grow on the earth, he realized that he needed to do something much more far reaching than simply killing one here or another there. He needed to do something that would corrupt the entire human species.

By the time we get to chapter six of Genesis, this is exactly what Satan has worked to accomplish. However, we are first introduced to Noah in chapter five. Here we read, *"Enoch walked with God; and he was not, for God took him.*

"25Methuselah lived one hundred and eighty-seven years, and became the father of Lamech.

"26Then Methuselah lived seven hundred and eighty-two years after he became the father of Lamech, and he had other sons and daughters.

"27So all the days of Methuselah were nine hundred and sixty-nine years, and he died.

"28Lamech lived one hundred and eighty-two years, and became the father of a son.

"29Now he called his name Noah, saying, "This one will give us rest from our work and from the toil of our hands arising from the ground which the LORD has cursed" (Genesis 5:24-29).

Noah came directly from the line of Enoch, making Enoch Noah's great-grandfather. In this chapter, we read that Enoch literally *walked with God* (v. 24). It was this righteousness that was passed down to Noah, and ultimately we learn that Noah was righteous in all his generations (cf. Genesis 6:9). Chuck Missler has indicated that from his study, we get the sense that the meaning here is that Noah's DNA had not been affected by cloning or cross-breeding.

If that is true, we must ask: who would have done experimentation with human DNA? It becomes clear then that in order for Satan to impact an entire race of people – all who lived – it would be much easier to change the DNA of the human beings that God had created. If Satan could do this, then the human genome, or DNA, would have been negatively affected and a Messiah would not have been able to have been born.

Is this what Satan did? At the beginning of Genesis 6, we read, "*Now it came about, when men began to multiply on the face of the land, and daughters were born to them, that the sons of God saw that the daughters of men were beautiful; and they took wives for themselves, whomever they chose.*

"Then the LORD said, "My Spirit shall not strive with man forever, because he also is flesh; nevertheless his days shall be one hundred and twenty years."

"The Nephilim were on the earth in those days, and also afterward, when the sons of God came in to the daughters of men, and they bore children to them. Those were the mighty men who were of old, men of renown" (Genesis 6:1-4). If we look closely, it seems as though somehow Satan was able to manipulate human DNA so that women gave birth to Nephilim. Though scholars do not agree on what the Nephilim were it seems clear enough that they were *different* from human beings. If this was not true, there would be no need to introduce the Nephilim. The word means *earth born*, and again, the fact that a new and different name was given to these individuals tells us that they were remarkably different from human beings.

Evil Rising

■ FROM THE GEOGRAPHIC ARCHIVES

Standing Tall in the Land of Genghis Khan

During the first of five expeditions to Mongolia, Roy Chapman Andrews photographed this seven-foot-five-inch man in 1922 in the capital city of Ulaanbaatar—

This photograph was never published in the magazine.

NATIONAL GEOGRAPHIC, DECEMBER 1996

We also note hundreds of years later, men like Goliath lived. The Bible tells us that Goliath was about nine feet, six inches, yet he was the smallest of his brothers (cf. 2 Samuel 21). So Goliath and his four gigantic brothers lived during the time when David fought Goliath. This might also explain why David chose *five* smooth stones, not just one, when he faced Goliath. He may have had five stones to deal with Goliath's brothers had they come out and attacked David after he slew Goliath, their brother. The point here is that something caused Goliath to be huge at nearly ten feet tall.

Goliath and his brothers were not the only ones. There is mention of a King Og ("Og" meaning "giant" in Hebrew) in Numbers 21 and 32. Deuteronomy 3:11 tells us that Og's bed was roughly 13 ½ feet by 6 feet. While it is possible Og simply *preferred* a large bed, chances are good that he was a type of giant as well.

Historian Augusta indicated that Caesar Maximus was 8 feet, six inches tall, which would make him the tallest Caesar to rule Rome. As shown on the previous page, even in modern times, we have people who are very tall. Even more recently, we see this within the NBA, where it is not unheard of for players to be well over seven feet tall. There have also been human footprints found in Kansas of an enormous size. If the tracks are genuine, the human who made the footprint would be around 25 feet tall. When the track was found, a bison track was located right next to it. There have been some very tall people in the world throughout time.

It is clear that Goliath, his brothers, and King Og were of a size that dwarfed the average person of that time. How did that happen? In fact, it is clear that when the Israelites first reached the Promised Land and had sent spies in to scout the land, most of the spies came back complaining about the fact that they felt like grasshoppers compared to those who were already in the land (cf. Numbers 13). While some commentators believe that the spies were exaggerating the size of the people simply because they did not want to go into the

Land, it seems clear enough that with Goliath being nearly ten feet tall with his brothers taller, there was probably not much of an exaggeration.

The point of all this is that it is reasonable to believe that with the Nephilim, Satan managed to mess with God's Creation so that the human DNA that God had created was changed. How it was done we do not know, but certainly Satan would have been capable of it. If he was capable of it then, he is capable of it now.

The technology that archaeologists have uncovered from ancient civilizations like Egypt, along with the biblical accounts of Goliath and others, shows us that what was once prevalent on this earth may yet again be so. That leads us to our next chapter.

6

Aliens, Demons, and Hybrids

It certainly seems possible that Satan, not content to simply allow things to play out, decided to involve himself in some witch doctoring of the human race. If he could successfully manipulate humanity's DNA, the chances of a Messiah being born would be greatly reduced. From all accounts, it appears that this is what he set out to do.

When we read about ancient civilizations, it becomes clear that there was a tremendous worship of a variety of gods. Eric Von Daniken's book *Chariots of the Gods* goes into great depth pointing to what he considers to be evidence that these gods were none other than aliens from outer space. He draws our attention to what appears to be vehicles that flew, piloted by these gods. Other things that appear to be watches worn on the wrist, as well as numerous other technologically advanced tools, seem to have existed among these ancient civilizations. Does Daniken have a point?

Certainly, in some ways Daniken's belief that these gods were aliens is on the right track, but he does not go far enough. This author believes that these aliens are nothing more than demons in disguise, using their knowledge like a master magician uses parlor tricks and sleight of hand to wow his crowd.

The difference, of course, is that these demons who pretended to be gods – those thought to be aliens by Daniken – actually were responsible for teaching the people of some of these ancient civilizations some of the dark arts, or the secret wisdom. These dark arts, also known as *magick* (with a "k"), is purely occultic in origin.

Imagine living in these ancient civilizations. Your mode of transportation is on horseback, or chariot, or walking. You begin to see things appearing in the sky that are scary at first. Because these beings arrive and communicate with you, you naturally begin to think of them as deities. Your natural reaction is to at the very least give them respect and at the most, worship them.

These beings are happy to receive your worship, and in exchange for it they will unveil mysteries that you did not know existed. Over time, your civilization moves way out in front of all the other civilizations due to what you have learned from these gods. Could it be that this is how God labeled what was going on at the time of Noah as continually evil? It is absolutely possible.

It is also interesting to note that Jesus spoke of the end of the ages just prior to His return as similar to the days of Noah and the days of

Lot (cf. Matthew 24, Mark 13, and Luke 21). What both of these time periods were noted for was their cruelty born of evil thoughts and intentions.

In both cases – Noah's days and Lot's days – people had learned to ignore God, doing whatever they wished to do. In Noah's case, we know that the Nephilim had something to do with it. If the Nephilim were offspring of fallen angels and human women somehow co-habitating (and who knows how that would have been done), creating an evil that pervaded society, it is also clear that during Lot's day, society was also exceedingly evil. The thing that people wanted to do the most was every sick sex act imaginable. Paul speaks about this in Romans 1, noting not only how bad it was, but the problems it causes for people, both spiritually and physically.

Both Noah's and Lot's days were characterized by evil – unavoidable and undiluted evil. It seems as though nothing was held back and people did whatever their minds conceived. Jesus tells us that this is what it will be like prior to His return. Do we have situations today in which demons are interfering with society in order to bring about their own goals? This author believes it.

During Noah's day, if these demons came to man appearing as something that people would classify as gods, it seems likely that they could and would do the same thing today, except instead of classifying themselves as gods, they are happy to be accepted as *aliens*.

For years, aliens were portrayed as evil. Many movies like *Forbidden Planet, Flash Gordon* and *Buck Rogers* serials, *War of the Worlds, The Day the Earth Stood Still*, and many others presented aliens that had far more power than human beings and when they came to this planet, their intentions were not good. They would come to destroy and/or take over the planet. This created a sense of fear among people so that when outer space was discussed, aliens were never normally seen as having good motives.

That slowly changed over time. It seems that the idea of aliens was introduced in a way that startled or even frightened people. By the late 40s, a new phenomenon began occurring within society that seemed to parallel at least some of the portrayals of aliens at the movies.

The world began hearing of abductions. People began speaking of tales of having been taken to a space craft and, while lying on a table, were poked and prodded. These were terribly traumatic to the individuals and they usually suffered from terrible nightmares and an unending fear that this would happen to them again.

Of course, when the world first learned of these abductions, they were generally thought to be the ravings of people who did not have all cylinders firing. Over time more people came forward to offer their own testimonies of personal experiences.

From that point, the productions Hollywood produced began showing aliens in a more favorable light. We were introduced to new alien individuals who were not all that bad after all. On television's *Star Trek*, Mr. Spock became a household name. Interestingly enough, Spock was a hybrid, born of human and Vulcan parents.

Close Encounters of the Third Kind, Star Wars, ET and more began showing aliens as lovable creatures that had been simply misunderstood by human beings for far too long. This created the necessity by the aliens to create situations where they could introduce themselves to human beings in a controlled setting.

Interestingly enough, the world began to see aliens in a different light. Groups were formed and looked for opportunities to make contact with our new outer space friends. People like Jacque Vallee wrote books on the alien phenomenon and spent his life researching them. He had come to believe, however, that these aliens – whatever they were – were not truly friendly, but were simply masquerading.

He came to understand them not as interplanetary travelers, but inter-dimensional beings, which simply moved from their dimension to ours at will. Vallee became convinced of their evil intentions.

Yet we have many today who believe that these beings not only exist but are actively engaging in mental or spiritual conversations with chosen human beings. George Green is one such individual who talks about his contacts with Raelians, which are a branch of aliens. According to Green, there are some interesting things about this planet that the aliens have clued him and others in on.

Earth is what is known as a prison planet because of the various cultures that have all been thrown together. We were created by Elohim, which is not the God of the Bible, but really a group of alien entities that gave us life. Their goal was to have us live peacefully, but obviously this has not been the case.

One of the big problems, says Green, is that this planet was made to only hold 500 million people, *total*. Obviously, we have gone way past this number so the aliens – from Pleadians, to Raelians, to Umos, to everything in between – have found it necessary to get involved in our process.

In order to reduce the population down to 500 million, we would need to eradicate nine-tenths of the present population. That is a lot of people! So what is the elite of this earth doing about it? They are making plans to do just that in a variety of ways.

Of course, this again sounds like science fiction, but one has to wonder how this cannot be true, since it appears to be believed by a growing number of individuals throughout the globe. Green himself is one who is working or at least looking toward the end of much of the earth's population. Though not considered to be among the earth's elite (the Illuminati), Green nonetheless states on a number of videos on the Internet that he routinely hears from the Raelians.

They send messages to him and provide him with information that helps him make decisions about a variety of things.

George Green certainly sounds intelligent and not at all off his rocker. The one thing that is disturbing, however, is how quickly and actively he accepts what is told to him by these entities. He never seems to question them or their activities, believing that they are helping us achieve what we were created to achieve.

In this way, everything becomes amoral. There is nothing immoral because that is all relative. At one point in the video this author watched, the interviewer pointed out that she was aware that not all aliens are "good," and that some have "negative" intentions. Green responded that it was all relative to their particular quest or purpose, to which the interviewer acquiesced.

It appears that once aliens are introduced into the equation, absolute right and wrong exit. From that point on, it is simply what needs to be done to fall in line with the proscribed mission. Killing then is not morally wrong if it fulfills the purpose for which this planet was intended.

This is exactly why people like Adolf Hitler are able to do what they do without remorse. They see the world and universe differently than most do. They see themselves as being above the laws that humanity has created. In effect, the global elite also see themselves above created laws. Those laws are for the common, lower class person, but not for those of certain bloodlines.

Green relates in the video that he was invited to take a very important government finance position during the next coming presidency. He then asked who the next president was going to be, and he was told Jimmy Carter. At that point, he had not even heard the name yet.

Green was also told that his position would work with and be under Ted Kennedy. As he introduced himself to Kennedy, he was told how much he would love the job because of all the money he would oversee and all the beautiful women he would meet.

At that point, Green says that a beautiful young woman walked into the room and Kennedy immediately noticed her. He then stated that he needed to go to bed with her. Green objected by stating that the girl was his daughter and she was only fourteen, to which Kennedy responded that he did not care about that.

The reality is that the world's elite have always lived under a different set of rules and those rules only apply to them. The rest of us simply get by having to follow the rules that they do not.

Green ultimately chose to not accept that particular job offer, but recounts his adventures since then and before. He talked of having top secret clearance in the military and not only seeing outer space alien craft, but bodies of aliens as well. He speaks of learning about the elite's plan to bring about war that will destroy much of the earth's population.

One of the wars was supposed to have taken place in early 2000, but has not. He admitted that things are behind schedule.

Green also talked about trans-humanism and *synthetics*. We will delve into these subjects later on in this book. They are certainly fascinating, but will also be seen as purely science fiction to many people.

7

One-World Government

George Green speaks of a number of highly interesting things in a number of videos found on the Internet. He explains, for instance, why there not only *needs* to be, but *will* be a total financial collapse. The reason will likely not surprise anyone who has already researched the subject with an open Bible.

A financial collapse is the surest and easiest way to bring about a new world order. It cannot be done without a financial collapse. People need to see that the "old" monetary system of paper currency no longer works. They need to have the rug pulled out from underneath them. Green advocates – as do a good many people today - investing in silver and gold. He notes that wherever he goes, he carries $5,000 with him in gold and silver coins. He can do that with as little as five to ten coins, so it is not as if he is weighted down with gold such that he cannot walk.

Going through an airport is not a big deal because he simply takes the coins out of his pocket and places them in the coin dish with his keys. The dish goes through the x-ray machine and since they simply look like coins, no one is the wiser.

Green as well as many others says the collapse will come, and from it will rise not only a new form of currency, but a new form of government. In order for the elite to bring about their plans, which are in effect the plans that they believe they have been given by aliens who created us and this planet, major things have to break down. This will create a populace that is drawn even more dependent upon governing bodies.

Very few people in this world honestly know how to live off the grid. There are few people who could sustain themselves in the mountains, for instance. We see on TV shows about people who can be dropped anywhere in the world and survive. They can make a meal out of certain types of grasses, berries, frogs, and snakes. The rest of us would likely die trying.

The elite have essentially formed a system whereby all people under them have become indebted to it. For so long people have learned to depend upon the systems in place that once these systems are gone, they will not know what to do. They will demand that our collective leaders come together and offer us solutions. This the elite will be more than happy to do because it plays right into their hands.

It will be extremely easy for the elite to open up their playbooks with the plans that they have known about and have been attempting to implement for years and put those plans into effect. They may certainly endeavor to appear as though the terrible situations have taken them by surprise just as much as it has taken the world by surprise, but the truth is that they will be lying.

What is coming down the pike is what the elite have planned for and want to happen. In fact, they need it to happen in order that they will survive.

Green spoke of a number of deep underground bunkers in places like Australia and elsewhere in which the elite will house themselves when a nuclear war occurs. There, protected from the fallout, they will squirrel themselves away until it is safe to appear above ground, all the while continuing to direct the events of earth from their secret and safe lairs.

Of course this all sounds once again as complete science fiction. If you ask Jesse Ventura, he will tell you that the bunkers exist. Others are of the same mind. Do they exist, and if so, do they exist for the purposes of the elite? Without actually seeing one and hearing or reading the plans, it is impossible to know, so it is one of those situations in which we simply choose what we believe to be the case.

Is it really all that difficult to believe that a group of individuals (call them *Illuminati*; call them *elite*, call them something else) exist who have plans to take over the world? Is that really science fiction? Not if we consider the fact that starting with Nimrod of Genesis 11, there have always been people who want to dictate to others and to the whole world if they could.

In fact, there have been a handful of individuals who have come close to ruling the entire world. Whether it was Alexander the Great, Nebuchadnezzar, or the Roman Empire, there have been and always will be (until Jesus returns) people who want to have the final word, the final authority over all others.

Even on a much smaller scale, Idi Amin, Saddam Hussein, Mussolini, Hitler, and others have endeavored to rule over people and have done so with a rod of iron. They were brutal beyond measure, and that is often the case when evil, fallen people take the reins of a society. Nothing is sacred at that point, except their own desires. Everything else is completely secondary.

If Saddam Hussein could have, he would have conquered the entire world. The same could be said of Hitler, Mussolini, Lenin, Stalin, and others. Their goals were to be top dog, answering to no one. These men were empowered by demons and each one of them has played an important part in ushering in the coming New World Order (NWO). Each dictator has done his part to bring this world toward a more unified end.

The global elite presently work together to achieve their own goals. They look to the future when they believe their god Satan will rule supreme and them directly under him. To them, it is opposite of what the Bible teaches about God and Satan. They see Satan as being the misunderstood and temporarily vanquished king, who will one day take his rightful place as leader of this world. The elite will be rewarded according to what they have done to help bring that about.

Though the global elite work together now, there will come a time when they will no longer see all common people as their enemy. That is the case now, which is why they can remain united. However, once the enemy has been dealt with and there is nothing else that stands in their way to keep them from absolute rule, they will of necessity have to turn on one another. This is always the case.

Consider the fact that the Antichrist, who is likely alive right now and waiting for his preordained appointment to rise to the top of the elite pool, will one day turn on three of the kings of the future and kill them. The remaining kings will give their allegiance to the Antichrist because they value their lives.

Where does it teach this? It is not from some global elite's playbook. It is the book of Daniel that reveals this information to us, and because it is in the Bible, we can be assured of its accuracy.

In Daniel chapter seven, Daniel relates the vision he had during the time of Belshazzar, king of Babylon. Here, Daniel outlines for us the rise of certain kingdoms and how each would eventually be supplanted by the next.

Daniel speaks of four beasts, each beast representing a different and successive kingdom. There was the lion-like eagle that represents Babylon. The kingdom after that was the Medo-Persian, represented by the bear. The Hellenistic kingdom, led by Alexander the Great, followed that and is represented by the leopard. Following this kingdom is a kingdom that is completely different from the others.

It turns out that this fourth kingdom was the Roman Empire. What is interesting is that since the beginnings of the Roman Empire, even though that empire is no longer, it has essentially evolved into a number of things.

When the Roman Empire first began to break down, it did so into two divisions: the east and the west. From there, it has continued to change, and in a strong sense is still evolving. What we have today is the east and west axis of power, comprising most of the world. The east is the Asian part of the world and we are aware of the fact that China's economy is important to not only that part of the world, but the entire world. In the west, the United States holds a very important part of the world's economy.

Once these two axes of power fall, the need for a one-world government will exists. Interestingly enough, the Bible indicates that once the world moves into a one-world government it will be divided up into ten sections, overseen by one individual per section (cf. Daniel 7). This is not to say that the world will cease to be one. It simply means that after becoming one, the need to section the world into ten areas will exist in order that it will become easier to control things. It will be no different than any large company that has a CEO with a board of advisors. Each of those advisors would be in charge of one aspect or area of the company and would report to the CEO.

Once the world is broken up into manageable sections, it will be at this point the Antichrist will make his move to the top. Daniel states: *"I considered the horns, and, behold, there came up among them another little horn, before whom there were three of the first horns plucked up by the roots: and, behold, in this horn were eyes like the eyes of man, and a mouth speaking great things"* (Daniel 7:8).

The ten horns referenced above refer to the ten sections of the world controlled by one king or ruler over each. Notice though that there are ten horns, but Daniel then sees "another little horn." One of the first things this "horn" does is to get rid of three of the other horns ("three of the first horns plucked up by the roots"). It is the Antichrist and he is making his bid for top man.

Daniel tells us that this horn had eyes like a man and a mouth that boasted about himself. This is the Antichrist and he will rise to the top under which all other individuals (including the global elite) will live.

So where are we in this picture? Obviously, as this is written, the world's economy has not collapsed, yet one has to wonder how far off that is before that occurs. Since the economic collapse must occur before the one-world government and ten divisions, it is safe to say that it is still before us, though we do not know how much time we have before those things occur.

It is probably safe to say that when the world's economy does collapse, the global elite will move quickly to secure their place as leaders of the world. It will of course make sense that once the monetary collapse happens, moving the world toward a one-world government will take place quickly as the global elite is seen as the world's savior. Unfortunately, it will be solely due to the global elite that the world's economy has collapsed in the first place.

This seems to be all part of their plan to bring this world in line with the revelations they have received from entities outside of this world. The global elite do not care about anyone outside of their own circle. Certainly they need workers, so many people will need to continue to exist on this planet, but they will be to fulfill the needs of the global elite. Can you see the global elite actually doing physical labor of any kind? That would not work, hence the need for additional people. Who will remain? Only those who will be absolutely loyal to the global elite and their plans will remain, of course. Anyone else will be easily removed...from this planet.

8

One-World Religion

You would think that a future new world order has no need for religion, and in many ways, you would be correct. There is no real need for it, yet there will be a strong desire for it.

Like many things in the NWO, there will be one way of doing things, through a one-world government. A one-world religion will serve the ultimate purposes of the NWO because the global elite worship Satan in some form or other, whether they actively do so or not.

It must be remembered that the chief goal of Satan according to Isaiah 14 and Ezekiel 28 is to *be worshipped* above God. It is to this end that he has designed his plans. If he can be worshipped above God, then he will have proven that he is *better* than God. If he can prove that he is better than God, then it would be possible for him to *overcome* God.

It is because of this that everything he does stems from this point. When he tempted Jesus in Matthew 4, his goal there was to get Jesus to worship him. Sure, Satan would have been happy if Jesus had simply sinned by turning rocks into bread, but ultimately, he wanted Jesus to worship him.

Had that occurred, then he would have been successful in raising himself *above* God. Does that make sense? In other words, John opens his gospel by telling us that Jesus (the Word) was in the beginning with God as God. Throughout the gospels and the New Testament, we are told repeatedly that Jesus was and remains God.

As God, Jesus humbled Himself and was born into this world, growing up without ever sinning. He finally came to the point of sacrificing Himself for our sins. Jesus is God in the flesh.

Satan knew and knows this, which is why he tried to get Jesus to worship him. Satan had promised to raise himself above God's throne, and it was because of that boast that sin was found within him. The power and authority that went to his head caused him to rebel against God and he came to believe himself to be something he was not, nor will ever be.

But if he could just get Jesus – God in the flesh – to bow to him, he would have proven God wrong and literally have raised himself above God. This he of course failed to do, but this tells us that Jesus was and remains God. This is at least one reason why the deity of Christ is so very important and cannot be denied.

Though Satan knew that Jesus was and remains God, he works very hard to cause people to doubt that and once they doubt it, salvation eludes them, because if it is denied that Jesus is God, then Jesus Himself is denied. In essence, those who reject Christ's deity wind up rejecting Jesus because He is God. Rejecting Jesus' deity means rejecting God.

So Satan has spent centuries and centuries setting up a situation where he will be worshipped *above* God. He failed to cause Jesus to willingly worship him, but he keeps trying. He works hard to cause normal people and believers to worship him, but that is still not good enough. In fact, even when the entire world worships him, it will still not be good enough because even when the entire world worships him, while *they* may be worshipping him above God, Satan will not be elevated above God through that worship. It may satisfy his ego, but it will not fulfill his promise that he will raise himself up above God's throne.

Satan will certainly take that though because he is egotistical. He wants and needs to be worshipped. While simply being worshipped is not as good as being worshipped *above* God, it will do for the time being.

So during the future time when the world literally becomes one, then the global elite section things off into ten areas, the Antichrist will rise to the top and install himself as the most important man on earth.

Satan allows this because it moves everything towards his purposes. The one thing that Satan will *not* allow during this time and into the Tribulation is the worship of anyone other than himself. When people eventually bow to the Antichrist, directed by the coming False Prophet, their worship of him will be accepted by Satan. Because Satan empowers Antichrist, worship of Antichrist will be worshipping Satan. That will be the allowed worship. Nothing else will be acceptable and that is why at one point during the Tribulation, martyrdom will prevail as an all-out war on those who believe only in the One, True God (cf. Revelation 6:9-11; the Fifth Seal).

The New Age movement has long taught that we are all gods deep within and it is a matter of unlocking that deity. Once unlocked, we gain full authority over our own life, allowing us to create whatever we want our life to become. Of course, since within the New Age movement people are taught to worship themselves as gods, this is something that Satan approves of because a person who worships him or herself does not worship the One True God of the Universe. They are also indirectly worshipping Satan.

This lie that Satan first used against Eve and Adam in their paradise called Eden is something that has worked so well for fallen creatures that he has not had to use anything else. He simply uses the same lie in new clothing. He may change what it looks like on the outside, but in reality, it is the same worn out lie and people continue to fall for it in droves. Why use something else when this one lie has worked for thousands of years?

Folks, we are not, nor have *ever* been, any type of god. We are not self-created, but were created by God to reflect His image – His capacity for thought and reason, along with the ability to *feel* a myriad of feelings and emotions. Compassion, sympathy, empathy, sadness, hatred and possibly most importantly, *love*. Since the fall, humanity's ability to feel various emotions has been seriously tainted. It has become impossible to trust our emotions as guides.

Too many people continue to rely on their feelings to make decisions. Even Christians fall into this trap and because of it wind up making terrible decisions at times in their life. How many times have we heard some well-meaning Christian say "I feel as though the Lord wants me to do thus and so"? God does not generally lead us through the venue of feelings and emotions because they are not reliable.

God primarily leads us through intellect and knowledge based on His holy Word.

Consider the fact that there are so many professing Christians today who change their belief about one theology or another based on their *feeling*. It is not uncommon to hear comments like, *"I just don't feel that God would send people to hell for all eternity,"* or *"I feel that because God loves all people, all people will ultimately be saved,"* or something else.

The truth remains that if God's will is based on the way we feel about it, then what we have is a God that changes. We can try to argue that we now see things differently and that has caused us to change our opinion about something God has stated in His Word. However, this does not let us off the hook.

The reason we usually change a position on something as important as salvation or some known sin is usually due to the fact that *our outlook has changed*. We begin to place less emphasis on God's Word because maybe we no longer see it as being completely true. Maybe, we think, while God oversaw the writing of it, He was more into *concepts* than actual verbiage.

In other words, our opinion of God's Word changes so that eventually we begin to see our own intellect and reasoning abilities as being more important and more true than God's Word. We can do this by reasoning that the culture of Jesus' time was one culture, but ours is a different culture. Therefore, God would not expect the same things of us today that He expected then, would He?

People have all sorts of ways of justifying their actions, attitudes, and verbiage. This then creates a situation where that person is their own highest authority. They might not even realize it, but they have already begun walking down the path labeled "I am god." When this happens, it is not long before we begin to make excuses for everything in God's Word with which we disagree, so that we can do what we want to do without feeling as though we are breaking God's law.

God never wants us to set our intellect aside. We need to recognize, though, that our intellect is never even close to God's. Who among us can honestly comprehend (not simply know) the Trinity? I know that, according to Scripture, there is one God. There has always only been one God and there will always and forever only be one God.

I also know from Scripture that this one God is composed of three distinct personalities; the Father, the Son, and the Holy Ghost. I know and understand that truth, but do I absolutely comprehend it? Not in this life. It is precisely for that reason that many reject the idea of a triune God. They cannot wrap their brains around it, so they reject it.

For instance, Jehovah's Witnesses accept the idea of one God. There is only one God to them, but that God is not triune. The Jehovah's Witness understands that concept as *three separate gods*, of which the Bible clearly teaches against.

This author can certainly agree that there is only one God, not three individual gods, as Jehovah's Witnesses, Muslims, and others believe this is how the Christian understands it. The trouble is, in the case of the Jehovah's Witness, they try so hard to reject any inherent deity of Jesus that they wind up actually contradicting themselves. Case in point is John 1:1, which states, *"In the beginning was the Word, and the Word was with God, and the Word was God."* Jehovah's Witnesses translate that verse in their New World Translation as *"In the beginning was the Word, and the Word was with God, and the Word was **a** god."* (Emphasis added) Now, if Jehovah's Witnesses teach that there is only one God, then how can there be any other type of god, as they seem to teach with their translation of John 1:1? Either Jesus is God or He is not God. Jehovah's Witnesses tell you that Jesus is not God, but He is *a* god, something that contradicts their own beliefs and teachings about the Trinity.

As things begin to fall into place, the idea of enforcing a one-world religion will not be that important at the start. However, as things take shape and settle in, the rise of the Antichrist will also usher in the rise of a one-world religion with Antichrist being the object of that worship.

Not only will the global elite extend their allegiance and worship to Antichrist, but those within Islam will have little problem accepting him as the Final Mahdi. According to Islam, this Final Mahdi will lead them to victory over those outside Islam (Christians, Jews, and others). This is their belief and so we can see that the entire world will move toward a time of oneness, both in government and religion.

Hell Hath Fury!

We have seen a few of the things that are being perpetrated by the forces of evil that will usher in the time of horrendous evil; evil that this world has never experienced. Currently, there are those among us who believe they are in nearly constant communication with aliens. These aliens – they believe – want to help us, and because of the fact that human beings cannot get along, have felt the need to step in and help us through the process.

We have seen that the global elite believes that the plans and messages they have received from these aliens is the roadmap of the future that will usher in (for them) unprecedented peace and reward.

We have also noted that as the world becomes one, forced to do so after an economic crash like nothing this world has ever seen, one individual will rise to become the final dictator in Satan's plan to imprison all people and overthrow God.

Beyond this, we have highlighted the possible links between what occurred during the times of Noah and Lot and what the end of this age will be like just prior to the Lord's return. In this chapter, we would like to spend a bit more time concentrating on the tone of this planet once hell begins to release its fury.

This author believes that at least part of the reason we are seeing an increase in unexplainable crime is due to the preparations that hell is making for its final assault on this planet's population. Daily we seem to read of instances and situations occurring throughout this world that have no plausible explanation.

For instance, why did 50-year-old Julie Schenecker recently decide to calculatingly kill her 13-year-old son as they drove to soccer practice, and upon her return, kill her 16-year-old daughter who was working on her computer? Her excuse was that her children "were mouthy." Is this a reason to take life? It is no reason.

We are learning that there were a few instances in Schenecker's past that are troubling. Just a few weeks prior to these killings, the daughter called police to complain that her mother had hit her and had done so about a month earlier as well. Just days later, the mother was involved in a car accident in which police believe her ability may have been impaired by drugs.

According to neighbors, this was a perfect family, but of course, looks have always been deceiving. How many times have we heard or read about someone who simply goes off like a rocket, but by all accounts prior to that was a quiet person who bothered no one? Apparently, Schenecker's murderous actions were the result of premeditation.

She wrote at least one note prior to picking up the gun she had purchased, complaining about the three-day waiting period from purchase to pick up, something she said would *"delay the massacre."*[7] On the day she was arrested, it was clear from a video of the event that Schenecker was suffering from something. Her eyes wide, as she was escorted in handcuffs with a law enforcement official on each side of her she exhibited signs of shaking or tremors. There simply seems to be something terribly wrong with Schenecker with which a three-day waiting period did not do anything to curtail her desire to kill her own children.

What are we referring to here, demonic possession, mental disorders, or something else? At this point, certainly no one knows for sure, but it seems clear enough that no one in their right mind takes the time to deliberately plan to kill their own children in cold blood.

Of course, we have the case of Jared Loughner, who gunned down a number of people including Congresswoman Giffords. In this case, Loughner was known to have mental problems that had gone untreated.

Over the past number of years, there has definitely been an increase in terrorism and terrorist-related crime. It is also no longer sequestered to one particular area of the globe either. Who in the United States or the world will ever forget the 9/11 attacks in which nearly 3,000 people were killed?

Wars and rumors of wars are also on the climb. With everything that has been happening in the Middle East, the entire world watches to see what will occur next.

Ethnic cleansings still occur, one culture fights to kill another culture. Persecution of Christians worldwide is on the rise with more Chris-

---

[7] http://www.msnbc.msn.com/id/41470258/ns/us_news-crime_and_courts/

tians being killed in this century than in all the previous centuries combined.

We know of the drug-related crime and murder that routinely occurs in Mexico, with at least some of it spilling over into America. Recently, a missionary husband and wife team who were in Mexico, where they had ministered to the people of Mexico for years, experienced being shot at for what was most likely the drug cartel's desire for the truck they were driving. In the process, the wife was shot in the head and died.

It seems as though people across the globe are simply either going or doing insane things that speak of a new, terrible threat to humanity that seemed not to exist prior to the present. Take for example one father in Papua New Guinea. Residents awoke to the sounds of a screaming baby, and as it turned out, the father was *eating* his newborn son! Known to the community as an individual who had regularly abused drugs, this man was eating his child during what was described as a sorcery initiation ceremony. *"Locals are saying the man was carrying out a sorcery ritual, or initiation, to become part of some sort of special society," [a local police commander] said.*

"The suspect has a long history of drug abuse and we are not surprised something like this has happened.

"A few years ago, he went crazy in what we believe was due to the effects of drugs," he said.

"In 2009, it was estimated at least 50 people were killed that year in sorcery-related murders in sudden or unexplained deaths in isolated communities."[8]

If we look back on recent history, we see a number of door-opening events that changed the face of society worldwide. Consider Elvis

---

[8] http://www.smh.com.au/world/man-caught-eating-baby-20110205-1ahch.html

Presley. His dancing was seen as immoral because of his gyrating hips that certainly in some sense imitate sexual movements during intercourse. Elvis himself really seemed to have no clue why there was such uproar, and that may well be true. The fact of the matter is that it drove people – especially young girls – to a state of excitement that heretofore did not exist.

We know of the strange sexual proclivities that occurred in Elvis' life later on in his career. We also know Elvis as a man with a beautiful baritone voice and whether he was singing "You Ain't Nothing But a Hound Dog" or "Amazing Grace," his voice had the ability to make women swoon. Knowingly or not, Elvis' antics and gyrations on stage opened the door to more overt sexuality in society.

The Beatles are a group of young men that will be remembered as long as human history exists. When they flashed onto the world's music scene, songs like "I Wanna Hold Your Hand" were the norm. These were simple songs, which spoke of something as innocent as holding the hand of a loved one. Parents did not like the haircuts, the pointed-toe shoes, or the fact that girls everywhere were fainting at the sight and sound the Beatles created.

It was not long before the innocent-sounding lyrics gave way to lyrics that had been laced with Transcendental Meditation concepts and worse. The Beatles' *Sgt. Pepper's Lonely Hearts Club Band* album was simply weird. It was an experimental concept album released by the Beatles in June of 1967. Since then, it has remained as a highly acclaimed album, having won four Grammys in 1968. Pepper is said to include references to recreational drug use and of course, the cover itself includes images of many famous celebrities from all walks of life; people like Carl Jung (psychiatrist), W.C. Fields (actor), Sigmund Freud (psychiatrist), Aldous Huxley (writer, atheist), Marilyn Monroe (actor), Aleister Crowley (occultist), Karl Marx (communist), Sri Paramahansa Yogananda (Hindu Guru), and many others. John Lennon

Part of the Woodstock crowd in 1969 where drugs and sex were rampant.

is said to have wanted to include Adolf Hitler and Jesus Christ, but these two individuals did not make the album.

We know that since that time, not only drugs, but transcendental meditation (TM) became big in America. Since the Beatles were so popular, what they did was often mimicked in society.

It was not long before more artists and groups came on the scene that seemed to extol the virtues of recreational drug use, free sex, and communal living. In one strong sense, Woodstock promoted all three. Taking place in 1969 on a 600-acre farm in upstate New York, the Woodstock festival attracted 500,000 concert goers where 32 musical acts performed.

What began as an innocent foray into love and drugs soon became an integral part of society – a dangerous part of society. It has become clear that drug use in society causes problems. It has become equally clear that once something finds its way into society, there is no removing it. Recreational drug usage is a major societal problem that continually fuels the drug cartels of Mexico and elsewhere, leaving untold death and mayhem in its wake. There is really nothing that can be done to completely remove drugs from the population. One of the worst drugs to infect society of late is methamphetamine because it is so addictive. At all costs, addicts will do whatever it takes to feed their habit, even if that means lying, cheating, stealing, or even killing.

Drugs are known to change the brain patterns. Any drug can do that; however, drugs that are generally prescribed by a qualified physician are meant to help, not hurt. Drug abuse is where people get into problems because they take the person beyond the intents of medical science.

For instance, a needed prescription for cortisone can help the body heal. Too much cortisone can damage internal organs and possibly kill. Other steroids can aid in healing but steroid abuse can lead to certain problems. There is no concrete evidence that steroid use has caused cancer and in fact, in a number of cases, patients with HIV have been treated with steroids with excellent results. People that should have died due to the AIDS virus 15 years ago or more are still living and look absolutely normal in weight and health.

The problem though is drug abuse. Recreational drug use is not treating anything. People engage in recreational drug use because they want a high. They want to feel powerful, invincible, or simply more alive. This type of unregulated drug usage can and has killed many. People feel invincible because these drugs change the brain wave patterns, chemically forcing the brain to do what it might normally do, but in far greater measure. This puts a tremendous weight on the body's neural system, and after a while it will need to go to the opposite extreme in order to allow the body to recoup. Constant illicit drug use can create permanent problems.

Additionally, when these brain wave patterns are changed, it is very possible to open the door to spiritual beings in the other dimension. All of them, under the direction of Satan, roam about looking for open doors into people's lives.

Satan himself needed an open door in order to invade and begin to impact human society from within. This is exactly why he did what he did to cause Eve and then Adam to fall. Their disobedience to God brought about a major change in the world that will only be rectified with the physical return of Jesus at the end of the age.

It is with the willing permission given to Satan by Eve and Adam that Satan was able to wrest control of this planet and the air above it from our first parents. He was effectively given – through deceitful measures – the title deed to this earth.

While Jesus purchased it back (see Revelation 5) through His life, death, and resurrection, Satan is allowed to continue (for now) as if he still owns the earth. There will of course come a day when all of what Jesus accomplished on the cross will be fully put into effect and our vanquished foe will be actually and physically vanquished forever.

The bottom line is that Satan needed an invitation. His hordes of demons (fallen angels) also need an invitation to enter into the affairs of this world through human beings. There must be something that literally opens the door to these creatures, allowing them to wreak havoc in the lives of people and change the course of their lives and of society.

The drugs that change the brainwave patterns in the brain, even temporarily, cause people to lose some control over their thoughts and motor abilities. Losing control provides an open door that demons can and do take advantage of and that is clearly seen in the number of demonic possessions that occur throughout the world.

Not only are drugs a huge culprit, but anything that changes the brainwave patterns can be used against a person by a being from the other dimension. God did not intend for human beings to give up control of their thoughts. He did not want us to put our brains on idle, or give them over to the substances, ideas, or theologies that create emptiness or offer control to another.

Going back to the incident referred to earlier in this chapter, why would a father eat his own child? From the article, it is clear that the man was a drug abuser. If the enemy of our souls can find a way into a person's thinking through the open door of drugs, can that same enemy also come to control a person's thoughts and actions? We only need to look to Scripture for the answer to that question.

On one occasion, Jesus was approached by a man who was concerned about his son. Demons often literally threw the boy into the fire in attempts to kill him (cf. Mark 9). This is an obvious case where demons had somehow gained access into the boy's mind/life and were attempting to kill him.

Could this father that was eating his son have been *possessed* by demons? In today's world, it seems absurd to consider it, but the truth of the matter is that not only was this man a drug abuser, but he lived in a country where sorcery seems rampant. Sorcery is simply another form of devil worship and that will also open the door to Satan and his cohort. You get what you play for and in the case of this man and his child, we see no exception.

There are too many stories about how bad people can be to one another to reflect on here. If we consider what Russ Dizdar tells us about the Satanic Super Soldier and the potential there, it would appear as though the world has become a powder keg simply waiting for the lit match to set it off.

It is as if hell is desperately waiting to unleash itself onto an unsuspecting world in order to create the most heinous havoc and chaos imaginable. Pure evil seems currently only held back by the thinnest of curtains separating it from this dimension. That *will* change.

When we read passages in Scripture that teach us about the Tribulation (the first 3 ½ years) and the Great Tribulation (the second 3 ½ years), we quickly learn that during that time, evil will run rampant on this earth.

On at least one occasion, the pit of hell is opened and legions of demons are released to inflict pain but not death on the denizens of the earth. The narrative appears in Revelation 9:1-11 where John paints a picture of these demons (he calls them locusts) being so thick that it looks like smoke pouring forth from the pit!

One cannot help but wonder why this world is not now worse than it is and what is keeping it from becoming far worse? Certainly, this world has room to become even worse than what we see and hear today. What is it that keeps things at bay?

Paul tells us in 2 Thessalonians 2:7 that even though the mystery of iniquity is already at work in the world (during Paul's time and it is working that much harder during our time now), there is something holding that iniquity back, keeping it from vomiting itself onto the earth to its full capacity. Though Paul does not tell us who or what is holding back the evil (leaving many commentators to offer a variety of viewpoints), it seems clear to this author that it is the Holy Spirit working through the invisible Church.

Once the Rapture occurs, the Holy Spirit will no longer have the Church to work through. If you are one of those people who does not believe that the Rapture will occur before the start of the Tribulation, it is at least clear that whoever is holding evil back must move aside.

It is still likely to be the Holy Spirit who, at the appointed time, allows the full force of evil to enter this dimension from the spiritual realm.

If it is the Holy Spirit who presently holds back the full brunt of evil from penetrating this realm, imagine what it will be like when that same evil is allowed to enter unchecked. We can see that this world is in trouble. There is evil everywhere and it is obviously growing, pushing itself further into this realm.

Islam alone has increasingly brought greater evil into this world because Islam itself has grown. Radical adherents of Islam believe that by continuing to push themselves into other cultures, foisting their beliefs on those cultures, that they are winning more ground for Allah. The more ground they gain for Allah, the more evil they invite into this realm from the spiritual realm. It is a slow but consistent process that radical Muslims believe will ultimately usher in their age of peace.

During the Tribulation, there will be a time as mentioned where multitudes will die for their faith. They will be killed by the sword and other means (cf. Revelation 6). Revelation 20:4 specifically mentions those martyred through *beheading*, which seems to be one of the favored ways radical Muslims kill people when they are not blowing them up.

It seems as though not only does evil *not* take a holiday, but as time progresses toward the end, it will become so vast and unmeasured that it will strike terror in the hearts of people and will wind up killing people because their hearts will fail them (cf. Luke 21). That is terrible fear, unimaginable fear, yet it will happen and it will happen because of the increasing presence of the demons from hell into this realm.

Trans-humanism & Synthetics

Transhumanism is a word that is associated with the goal of exceeding known human limitations. In essence, it is the belief that what can be thought of in the brain can be physically conceived. It is the desiring of, and working toward, becoming *more* than simply human.

This can be done any number of ways, but mainly through technology. In the words of Francis Fukuyama, professor of international political economy at Johns Hopkins School of Advanced International Studies, trans-humanism is *"nothing less than to liberate the human race from its biological constraints."*[9] It is based on the idea that humanity has not yet reached its full potential and there is likely a good deal of room to grow before that goal is met.

---

[9] http://reason.com/archives/2004/08/25/trans-humanism-the-most-dangero

Many believe that this reaching toward the unknown limit will create the *posthuman*. *"The new species, or 'posthuman,' will likely view the old 'normal' humans as inferior, even savages, and fit for slavery or slaughter. The normals, on the other hand, may see the posthumans as a threat and if they can, may engage in a preemptive strike by killing the posthumans before they themselves are killed or enslaved by them. It is ultimately this predictable potential for genocide that makes species-altering experiments potential weapons of mass destruction, and makes the unaccountable genetic engineer a potential bioterrorist."*[10]

Of course, this is more science fiction-sounding than most would care to admit. Nonetheless, it is seen as plausible by a growing number of individuals and groups. In fact, Hollywood has once again provided us with their version of trans-humanism. Movies such as the *Matrix Trilogy, Terminator, Universal Soldier, Transformers, X-Men, Avatar, Tron, Spiderman, Green Lantern,* and of course many others portray trans-humanism in one form or another.

It is certainly no secret that director James Cameron's movie *Avatar* was essentially about trans-humanism. In the movie, one of the main characters was wheelchair bound, yet through the technological process of entering into another world and becoming his *avatar* (a representation of himself in another form), he literally ran faster and jumped higher. His connection with his alter-ego allowed him to live life on a completely different level than what he was capable of doing in a wheelchair. Of course, it is also no secret that James Cameron himself is an avid fan of New Age thought in which humanity can achieve whatever humanity sets out to accomplish. This train of thought is the hallmark of New Ageism and has permeated global society.

As part of this ongoing scientific process, a good deal has become artificial. Think of how far science has brought us. Years ago, people

---

[10] http://reason.com/archives/2004/08/25/trans-humanism-the-most-dangero

who lost a leg (or two) or arm in an accident or during war were relegated to a wheelchair, or hobbling around on some stiff-looking and likely very uncomfortable fake leg, or having to deal with a fake arm with hooks on the end of it. The fake leg served merely to help them get from one place to another. The fake arm allowed them to use basic utensils and simple things.

Now, high-tech legs are very lightweight and allow people to run at a fairly high rate of speed. The military has created a type of bionic exo-skeleton that allows military personnel to use far less energy to do the same type of work done now. We have all seen these types of creations in numerous movies and TV shows, but the idea that they have become actual working units in real life is something that we are just now getting used to seeing.

What is interesting is that while in at least some ways human endeavors are making life easier, we have not eliminated things like cancer or even the common cold. Beyond that, we have not been able to curtail or eradicate famine. Things like diseases and food shortages continue to exist. Sickness will be with us until we can find a way to inoculate everyone on the planet and ensure that they have enough food to not only survive, but to thrive.

So in spite of the advances made in the various scientific fields, we continue to lag behind in being able to feed the amount of people on this planet. As mentioned, those from other dimensions are telling us that it is because this planet was only designed to hold 500 million people and since the earth has a population of nearly 7 billion, we have really stretched earth's resources beyond what it is capable of producing. This is why for the elite and many within the New Age movement, the goal of having only 500 million people on this planet is something that is desirable.

This is one of the reasons that abortion will never again be outlawed and why homosexuality is something that the elite see as a good thing. They couldn't care less about any potential moral aspects of either abortion or homosexuality. They are merely selfishly seeing things from the viewpoint of what is sustainable.

Abortion eliminates the number of people on the planet by killing babies before they are born. Homosexuals do not necessarily procreate, but are more apt to adopt. In both cases, the population total does not increase. It is the heterosexuals that produce more people – people this world can ill afford to have because of the issue of sustainability.

Let's take a look at abortion for a moment. We know that prior to the Roe v. Wade decision by the Supreme Court, women found doctors who were willing to provide abortions illegally. They also found people who were not doctors willing to perform a very unsafe medical procedure that would abort the baby and possibly harm or kill the mother as well.

All of this played into the emotionally charged issue of abortion on demand. The feminists were squarely on one side of the issue, portraying themselves as an activist group concerned about the health and welfare of women. No mention was made of the unborn human life within the womb. In fact, many if not most feminists will tell you that no one really knows when life begins, and certainly it is naïve to suggest that a blob of fetal tissue could qualify as human life, nor could it survive outside the womb by itself. Of course, it could be argued that a full-term baby that arrives into this world to the joy of expectant parents would be completely unable to survive by itself outside the womb. A healthy baby needs parental care for months and years. So the argument that feminists like to vociferously toss at people who oppose them is without merit.

The abortion process is ultimately the cessation of life. Some prefer to call it the removal or expulsion of the fetus or embryo from the uterus. Seen in the latter way, it becomes very clinical, avoiding any mention of *life* with respect to the fetus or embryo. In fact, referring to it as an embryo seems to remove all vestiges of life from it; however, it can be clearly noted that an embryo is a *fertilized* egg. As such, life has begun because it is growing, and if all things go accordingly it will grow until such a time as it will no longer need to be inside the uterus.

Abortions are done in any number of ways. In some occasions, doctors reach through the vagina into the uterus, and using tongs, grab the baby by its head and pull. This process dislocates parts of the baby from itself, so in effect the baby is literally killed while being pulled apart. This is called a dilatation and suction curettage procedure (up to 14 weeks) and a dilatation and evacuation procedure (after 14 weeks). After 20 weeks, a number of procedures can be implemented to cause the death of the fetus, such as labor induction, prostaglandin labor induction, saline infusion, hysterotomy, or dilatation and extraction.

Whether the doctor vacuums out the baby, cuts it up and pulls it out, or uses another way, the end result is the same, which is the death of the baby. One way also used is the referred to *saline infusion*. This method is normally done during the *"2nd trimester, [and is] effected by replacing 200 ml of amniotic fluid with 200 ml of 20% saline solution, which stimulates uterine contraction, followed by fetal delivery in 12-24 hrs."*[11]

This process essentially burns the baby to death. Normally, fetuses that are delivered in such a way look like boiled lobsters with their skin being very red. In some cases, the skin is blackened as if the baby had caught fire in the womb.

---

[11] http://medical-dictionary.thefreedictionary.com/saline+abortion

One can only imagine the amount of pain that the baby experienced prior to death, though there are differing opinions regarding the incidence of felt pain.

> *"At 20 weeks, the fetal brain has the full complement of brain cells present in adulthood, ready and waiting to receive pain signals from the body, and their electrical activity can be recorded by standard electroencephalography (EEG)." — Dr. Paul Ranalli, neurologist, University of Toronto*

> *"An unborn baby at 20 weeks gestation 'is fully capable of experiencing pain. ... Without question, [abortion] is a dreadfully painful experience for any infant subjected to such a surgical procedure.' — Robert J. White, M.D., PhD., professor of neurosurgery, Case Western University*

There are any number of pro-abortion experts who disagree with the above quotes, believing that the lump of fetal tissue within the uterus is just that, a lump of fetal tissue incapable of feeling pain. Some of these individuals unfortunately include doctors, which in and of itself is a sad commentary on humanity – when doctors who are sworn to care for and sustain life if at all possible are at the forefront of removing life.

The sad fact of the matter is that if the abortion industry was not a money magnet, no doctor would be interested. The plain truth is that money drives the abortion industry just as it drives all forms of capitalism. If there is a way for people to make money, it will be exploited.

Evil Rising

Consider the Old Testament and the god Molech. Throughout the Old Testament, God tells the Israelites to avoid passing their children through the fires of Molech.

Molech was a god – born of Satan of course – for whom it was believed that by sacrificing your own child(ren) to it, you would be blessed with great wealth, health, or whatever else you were seeking. The way it worked was that during the ceremony, a large statue of Molech sat just behind an equally large pit. In the pit burned a bonfire, and as the baby or child was dropped into the fire a group of musicians would play to cover the sounds of the screaming child who was being burned to death.

Once placed in Molech's arms, the arms would slowly lean down toward the fire and the baby/child would simply fall into the pit. In effect, at least one of today's methods of abortion – the previously mentioned saline infusion – burns the baby alive until dead.

In 2 Kings 22-23, King Josiah was given a book found by the high priest. It turns out to be the book of Law from Moses and Josiah is beside himself with sorrow and angst. He decides that the book will be read and everything God said to do in it will be done. He was also very upset that a Sabbath to the Lord had not been observed for many years.

King Josiah then went around not only destroying all the "high places" (a phrase the Bible uses to describe the specific worship spots for all the false deities), but he has the pagan priests executed. These priests were in a position of authority and honor and instead of teaching the Israelites about God and His desires, they chose instead to teach the people about the various gods. This of course led the people into sin through spiritual adultery.

God rewarded Josiah by telling him that what He (God) was going to do because of His great anger He would not do while Josiah was alive. Josiah would live in peace and be carried to his fathers in death. The retribution that would pour out on the nation of Israel for their years of idolatry would be dealt with *after* Josiah died. In spite of Josiah's humble attitude toward God when he learned that Israel had not been doing what God had wanted, God's anger would only be turned away from King Josiah, not the nation itself.

The amount of children that were passed through the fire of Molech is unknown, yet we *do* know that this was a very common method of worship by many pagan nations of the Old Testament times. This practice was adopted by Israel because of King Solomon and the pagan priests that were appointed to their positions after him. Solomon's many marriages to pagan women (whether for political reasons or otherwise) prompted him to make these women happy by creating "high places" so that images of their gods could be set up for worship. This is certainly something that Solomon should not have done, yet he did. This brought God's righteous anger down on a nation that had been created by Him to be a light to the world. Instead, they fell into spiritual adultery through idolatry by worshipping gods that were made with human hands. This included sacrificing their young children to Molech by passing them through the fire.

This is a form of abortion – the killing of children – only in this case, they had already been born. In the case of today's abortive procedures, the life of the unborn is taken from them by people too selfish to see beyond themselves.

According to the Center for Bio-Ethical Reform, there are approximately 42 million abortions per year, with 115,000 performed each day throughout the world. In the United States alone, nearly 4,000 babies are aborted daily. Some other interesting facts include: *"52% of women obtaining abortions in the U.S. are younger than 25: Women aged 20-24 obtain 32% of all abortions; Teenagers obtain 20% and girls under 15 account for 1.2%."*[12]

There are other facts that are just as interesting. *"1% of all abortions occur because of rape or incest; 6% of abortions occur because of potential health problems regarding either the mother or child, and 93% of all abortions occur for social reasons (i.e. the child is unwanted or inconvenient)"* and *"An estimated 43% of all women will have at least 1 abortion by the time they are 45 years old. 47% of all abortions are performed on women who have had at least one previous abortion."*[13]

It seems clear that on one hand, while feminists want us to believe that women have the right to determine the outcome of every pregnancy, the tragic fact is that many abortions are performed on women who have already experienced an abortion. Certainly, while it is agreed that women should have control over their bodies, this should seriously be considered *prior* to becoming pregnant. Similarly, since women are unable to become pregnant without male sperm, the question of having control over their bodies becomes moot simply

---

[12] http://www.abortionno.org/Resources/fastfacts.html
[13] Ibid

because of this fact. Once the male sperm enters into the picture, consideration should be given to the growing life within the woman and the man from which the sperm came.

If women were more apt to use and insist on using some type of birth control, their egg would never become fertilized. If not fertilized, there would be no need for an abortion. As we have seen from the above facts, 93% of women who have abortions have them because the pregnancy is either unwanted or simply inconvenient. With this mindset, society is well on its way to becoming far more self-centered than ever. We have collectively decided that human life is only worth something when the fetus is actually planned and wanted. Apart from that, society says it is permissible to "sacrifice" the baby to the god of self.

God says it is not permissible, yet we do it anyway, killing millions of unborn children every year. How can we believe that God will continue to bless when we toss His moral code out the door?

If people would simply spend some time studying history to determine how much society has changed over the past five to seven decades, it would astound us. Yet, here we are in 2011 and it does not astound or even bother us in the slightest because we have been like the frog sitting in the pot of water that is slowly coming to a boil.

We have grown used to the changes in society and we have become hardened toward them. Abortion on demand is something that is completely acceptable today. Very few consider it to be a moral crime and in fact, many will tell you that it is necessary in most cases. Even in those cases where it is not necessary, the woman should always be the final arbiter of the choices that she makes with respect to her body and herself.

In today's society, while abortion on demand is something that even minors can have access to (at least in some states) without having to gain parental permission or even *tell* their parents, men are not so fortunate. The law says that my wife – should she be that type of person and thankfully she is not – could abort our child if she so desires without having to ask me or tell me. At the same time, my doctor would not perform a vasectomy on me without obtaining my wife's written consent. One can only stand back in amazement to realize that had my wife not wanted to sign the permission slip, a vasectomy would not have been done. Does anyone else see the absurdity here? The truth of the matter is that things have changed drastically in society – at least in western, democratic societies. Women are elevated, given complete control over their own bodies and are the only ones responsible for being able to make that decision in which, ultimately, a human life will be taken.

Yet for the man, a simple surgical procedure like a vasectomy which destroys no life at all requires the consent of the wife. The implausibility of this type of sexism goes unnoticed by most.

That aside, abortions today are merely modern-day sacrifices to Molech. Women spend time justifying their decisions to kill the growing life within them because of this reason or that, but the truth remains that the number one reason for killing the unborn child is due only to selfishness. There is no other reason. It is due to an unplanned pregnancy or the unwanted or inconvenient pregnancy.

If we are not killing unborn babies, we are spending time trying to create life in the test tube or clone animals. That is ironic, isn't it? On one hand, we dare not tell a woman that she has no right to kill a human being within her uterus, and on the other hand, scientists have been trying to create life for decades.

The tragedy is that it is this type of scientific interest in cloning that has caused some interesting hybridization. Even when cloning is not in the picture, selective breeding is with interesting results. For instance, cows in Belgium have been selectively bred so that the result

appears to be a cow on steroids. The Belgium Blues are bred by using only the largest bulls and cows to improve (or at least increase) the muscle mass. More muscle means more meat. It is difficult to know what that meat tastes like. Is it chewable or will your teeth or jaw break in the attempt to chew it?

This type of selective breeding goes back for centuries as man has always been enamored with trying to "improve" on God's Creation. The joke, though, is that God's Creation needs no improvement except for the future lifting of the curse.

Speaking of steroids, anyone who knows anything of steroids knows that it can and does create a massively powerful (albeit extremely odd-looking) human physique. However, at times people seem not to know when to quit, as is the case of the two men in the above photos. Someone should have taken away their steroids a long time ago, as they have simply become sideshow absurdities of gigantic proportions. How do either of these men buy shirts? Does the guy on the left have to have a built-in hood in each shirt? How about pants? How on earth do these guys walk without chafing the insides of their thighs off? The guy on the left walks around with his own pillow built into the back of his neck! That is simply asinine, yet he's smiling. Go figure.

The guy on the right isn't that much better. Can he scratch his back? Can he even scratch his nose without his pectorals getting in the way? Are all of his shoes minus the shoelaces? What is the matter with people? While it is realized that both of these men are literally *pumped* up and they do not normally look quite as bulky, the sad truth remains that they are both very large individuals even when they are *not* pumped and prepped for a body building competition.

We are seeing a growing number of movies and books that have latched onto the cloning and replicant idea that has permeated society. A number of recent movies stand out from the pack.

In *The Island*, starring Scarlett Johansson and Ewan McGregor, what we learn is that this island is where clones are housed. They are taught to look forward to the day when they leave the island. This event is seen as a graduation of sorts.

The truth of the matter is that when these individuals "leave" the island, it is to go into surgery so that their human counterparts can harvest parts from them. In other words, the clones are created for the sole purpose of providing harvestable parts for human beings from which they have been cloned. The clone in the movie – Ewan McGregor – discovers his purpose and escapes to save himself.

In a more recent movie, *Never Let Me Go*, "*life has a sell-by date, humans have a shelf life and death arrives in accordance with somebody else's schedule. You are a body to be plundered and mined for parts; get used to it.*"[14]

---

[14] http://www.guardian.co.uk/film/2011/feb/05/never-let-me-go-romanek

Evil Rising

Watch out...they're coming! You will be cloned! (On the set photo from *Invasion of the Body Snatchers*; Allied Artists Picture)

The idea of cloning, even as an aside, has been around for decades. Consider the movies *The Stepford Wives, Boys from Brazil, Gattica, Blade Runner, Sleeper,* and even the comical *Multiplicity*. These all deal with cloning, or replicants.

Even going as far back as 1956 with *Invasion of the Body Snatchers*, we have a movie that combines cloning with aliens from outer space coming to earth to take over. They do it by cloning humans and then taking their place as a complete look-a-like. You were fine...until you went to sleep. As soon as that happened, you could kiss your life good-bye.

Yet the movie also indicated that it wasn't so much that you died as you were simply taken over and absorbed into the new, *improved* alien form.

The *Jurassic Park* series also dealt with the cloning of dinosaurs with disastrous results. *The Fifth Element* includes a very technologically interesting scene involving cloning. Another movie, *Starman*, has Jeff Bridges as an alien who comes to earth looking very much human and winds up mating with Karen Allen, who becomes pregnant with...*who knows what? A Nephilim perhaps?*

The fact of the matter is that ever since Mary Shelley's *Frankenstein*, and probably long before that, people have been enamored with the concept of cloning life or creating it from scratch. Man has always wanted to play God, and if he can bring something to life that was either completely dead or never existed, he believes he will have become God. Cloning is a big step in that direction, but the truth is that cloning simply takes what already exists and duplicates it.

One gets the strong impression that it is ultimately Satan who is playing God here and using human beings to accomplish his goals of cloning and even attempting to create life from nothing. If Satan can accomplish that, he will certainly be seen as a god. He will never be able to do that, and in fact anything that he does accomplish is done only because God allows it and grants him the power to do so. This He does for His purposes.

However, Satan is working round the clock like a busy bee, attempting to pull the wool over as many human eyes as possible. In previous books, we have spoken about the various methods Satan has used and it seems as though there is something for everyone.

One of the most universal approaches that Satan has used is something the elite refer to as *Luciferianism*. In a nutshell, "*Lucifer symbolizes the cognitive powers of man, its potential to reach godliness by its own means. Luciferians believe that those attributes will eventually dethrone God and bring humans to their rightful place, as deities. This doctrine is fully embodied by humanism and its technological counterpart transhumanism. Clothed in an acceptable phrasing inside a Judeo-*

Christian context ("humanist" sounds less threatening and evil than "luciferian"), these philosophies are now part of popular culture. Through technological advancements and scientific breakthrough, extremely wealthy figures like Ray Kurzweil are publicly seeking to reach technological immortality."[15]

The interesting thing of course is that there are a myriad of images and statues that reference Lucifer in some form throughout the United States, Canada, and other places as well. Most people are not even aware of them, or simply look upon them as statues of Greek gods, born of mythology. However, it is very possible that Greek mythology stemmed from aspects of truth found in civilization thousands of years ago. In many cultures, there were reports of giants or weird-looking creatures. Can they all be myths? Can they not have some kernel of truth in them?

Consider the modern music movement. Having evolved from basic rhythm and blues to techno-pop to today's rap "music" and beyond, we have arrived at something that portrays a futuristic society with phases of trans-humanism built into it.

To reiterate, it would be helpful to remind ourselves of just exactly what trans-humanism is and what it hopes to be in the near future. *"Transhumanism is an international intellectual and cultural movement supporting the use of science and technology to improve human mental and physical characteristics and capacities.*

"The movement regards aspects of the human condition, such as disability, suffering, disease, aging, and involuntary death as unnecessary and undesirable. Transhumanists look to biotechnologies and other emerging technologies for these purposes. Dangers, as well as benefits, are also of concern to the transhumanist movement.

---

[15] http://vigilantcitizen.com/?p=329

"The term 'transhumanism' is symbolized by H+ or h+ and is often used as a synonym for 'human enhancement'. Although the first known use of the term dates from 1957, the contemporary meaning is a product of the 1980s when futurists in the United States began to organize what has since grown into the transhumanist movement.

"Transhumanist thinkers predict that human beings may eventually be able to transform themselves into beings with such greatly expanded abilities as to merit the label 'posthuman'. Transhumanism is therefore sometimes referred to as 'posthumanism' or a form of transformational activism influenced by posthumanist ideals.

"The transhumanist vision of a transformed future humanity has attracted many supporters and detractors from a wide range of perspectives. Transhumanism has been described by one critic, Francis Fukuyama, as the world's most dangerous idea; while one proponent, Ronald Bailey, counters that it is the 'movement that epitomizes the most daring, courageous, imaginative, and idealistic aspirations of humanity.'"[16]

This is scary that people believe that humans can arrive at a state of transformed humanity that would be far superior to what we have today. Yet it is becoming much more commonplace for artists like Rihanna, Beyoncé, Black-Eyed Peas, and others to promote a posthuman world where cyborgs, robots, replicants, cloned humans and improved humans rule the day. Of course, what we are not hearing is that the cost of *improvement* is going to be out of reach of the average individual.

Is that so far-fetched? Consider the cost of plastic surgery today, or other life-enhancement measures. Most people cannot afford them at all. These are only for the rich. How much more will products and procedures of the future cost people?

---

[16] http://vigilantcitizen.com/?p=3306

It is this author's belief that with the introduction and evolution of rap "music," the floodgates have once again opened to introduce more of the Illuminati's future plans. What is considered music is nothing more than raunchy poetry put to a beat. It seems like every time something new is introduced, it is done so in order to get society used to that fact so that when it actually happens in real life, no one is put off by it. The few that are put off will be quickly relegated to the category of antiquated, outdated, holdovers, unable to let go of the past in order to embrace the future. In case you are not aware, Christians – authentic Christians – fall into that category.

Consider something else. Who is it that "makes it big" in the world today? It seems as though there is no rhyme or reason. Aside from the narcissism deeply implanted in Hollywood, those outside of that inner circle are "made" because of something.

There are many celebrities who become celebrities due to the fact that they are connected with relatives who have been famous for decades. These individuals have a leg up – a big leg up – on the competition. People like Nicholas Cage, Gwyneth Paltrow, Drew Barrymore and many, many others, have gotten in the door of Hollywood because of their famous relatives.

Think of someone like Brad Pitt. He was not connected with anyone. How about Johnny Depp? Individuals like these are chosen for a reason and they often have very liberal ideas, goals, and beliefs. These things work well with liberal left-leaning Hollywood.

However, who *controls* Hollywood? Ultimately, it is the super-rich. Call them the Illuminati, the elite, or just call them über-rich. Someone has to control everything. So why then are people like Brad Pitt and Johnny Depp chosen? Simply because these are the people that are believed will make millions for their "handlers." While everyone connected with Pitt or Depp gets a piece of the pie, the largest slice does not go to the star. It goes to the top individual who oversees everything.

These are people like David Rockefeller, George Soros, and many others. They pull the strings behind the scenes, although Soros seems to have become more attracted to the limelight these days.

People like Brad Pitt and Johnny Depp are cogs, puppets, simply to be used by the puppet masters. As long as they play by that puppet masters' rules, they are fine. If they screw up they are out, because the people who make careers easily break them and have done so without batting an eye. The name of the game for the wealthy is to gain more wealth. They will use whomever they deem necessary or expedient at that moment. When their usefulness comes to an end, the individual is cast aside and a new flavor is found.

As long as the elite can use people like Rihanna, Beyoncé, Black-Eyed Peas, and others to take their message to the people, these artists will be successful. Once they decide they no longer want to play by the puppet masters' rules, they are no longer needed. To be in the position of artists like Rihanna, it requires a selling of the soul. Any moral code that these individuals might have been raised with is tossed, exchanged for the moral code of the elite.

People who are strong Christians don't make it in Hollywood and there is no reason why they should. There is nothing good in Hollywood that would want to make an authentic Christian be part of that scene. However, for those who became Christians *after* they achieved some level of fame, it quickly became clear that parts would be few and far between. Some do continue in the business, and it is likely that the Lord keeps them there to be a witness to the tremendous amount of people who are lost and going to hell.

By and large, Hollywood is an industry that sucks people in, uses them so that others will become even richer and then spits the same people out when they are done. Hollywood has no need to be concerned about people. That is not the motivating factor. The only motivating factor is *money*. That's it. Like Planned Parenthood and abortion, without money Hollywood would not exist. In both cases, the amount of money that passes from one person to the next is immoral, solely because of the impact on society today.

Hollywood likes to say that they simply mirror what already exists within society. That is a lie. What Hollywood actually does is work to instill within society the ideas and dreams they see, in order that those ideas and dreams become reality. The only thing that tends to mirror society is the documentary, and then only when it is produced with as much of an unbiased view as possible. Documentaries that are produced with a bias are not truly documentaries, but simply venues to slant the viewpoint of public opinion.

We are reaping what we have sown. The hens have come home to roost. Immorality leads to greater immorality. The doors are swinging wide open, leaving nothing to the imagination. The worst part is that through the process, people have become more hardened, incapable of exhibiting the human emotions with which God created us. It will only get worse.

11

The Illuminati

It is clear that for many people, the idea of the Illuminati is completely science fiction. It plays well on TV, in books, and in the movies, but in real life? How can that be? How can educated, intelligent people honestly give credence to the idea that a group of über-rich people from families from Europe could not only have a plan to take over the world, but have the ability to actually do it? Isn't this the fodder that fuels conspiracy theories?

It could very well be one of those good ol' fashioned conspiracy theories that plays well as a fairy tale but not in real life. Consider the fact that in the 1950s, Ayn Rand, an established author and philosopher, was given the order by Philippe Rothschild to put down the code of the Illuminati in book form as a work of fiction. The result – *Atlas Shrugged* – became a bestseller unintentionally. In the book lie the details of the plan that is said the Illuminati want to put into action in order to take over the world.

According to one source, the main characters in the book represent real entities or people. *"The main characters of Atlas Shrugged are code names for individuals or companies. The code is as follows:*

- *John Galt --- Philippe Rothschild*
- *Dagny Taggart --- Ayn Rand*
- *Dagny's brother --- The combined Railroad System*
- *Ellis Wyatt --- David Rockefeller*
- *Hank Rearden --- U.S. Steel, Bethlehem Steel*
- *Francisco D'Anconia --- Combined Copper Mines*
- *Galt, D'Anconia, and the Pirate --Rothschild Tribunal"*[17]

If this is true, then the book itself becomes far more than a work of fiction. It reveals a plan that has been in the works for quite some time as the Illuminati (or global elite) has sought a way to wrest control of this planet (by taking control of sectors of this planet first) from the people. The trick is to do so in a way that appeals to people's fears so that they are willing to give up that control, placing it in the hands of others.

Not wishing to leave any stone unturned, the global elite plan to control six areas of society:

1. Religious
2. Educational
3. Political

---

[17] http://www.kt70.com/~jamesjpn/articles/illuminati_plan.htm

4. Military
5. Economic
6. Social

In short, there is nothing that they will leave to chance and nothing that they cannot control. What becomes interesting of course are the details of the alleged Illuminati's plan. It covers the gamut and is detailed, at least as to its results:

- Remove the President and Vice-President
- Republican Successor throws election to Democratic
- Democratic President gets following laws enacted:
    - **Federal gun law** - removes all weapons away from citizens.
    - **Tax Exemption Status** - Removal of tax exemption from churches (This is House Bill 41)
    - **Genocide Act** - Making it a crime equal to murder to convert a person from one religion or faith to another.
    - **Presidential Martial Law Act** - This allows the President in time of "National Emergency" to suspend the Constitution, Congress, and the economic system. The President, in essence, becomes dictator of America.
    - **Anti-Hoarding Act** - This makes it a felony to have more than 30-days' supply of food, fuel or medicine stored up at one time.
    - **Anti-Business Acts** Equalization of Opportunity Act Fair Share Law Directive #10-289
- President Carter was able to get some of these laws enacted before leaving office.
- Plans for America: Make every person totally dependent on the government by:
- Creating a pseudo-fuel shortage and food shortage.
- Confiscating all guns.
- *Calling for "Helter Skelter"

- All trucks, trains, planes, and ships, except Military, will stop.
- An army of some 200,000 white prisoners and motorcycle gang members will create mass insanity in the streets by bombing church buildings, raping, murdering, and using other fear tactics.
- **Declaring Martial Law**. Activate the National Guard to keep order after the public cries out for any kind of help. There will be one policeman to every 5 people. Once this "National Emergency" is declared, it will never be cancelled.
- All countries except America will be sent against Israel for oil. The use of neutron bombs allows destruction of people while leaving all buildings, natural resources, and croplands intact. When the war is over, the world is to be ruled from Jerusalem.
- In addition:
  - 90% of the population of the US supposedly is to die in the 1st half hour of WWIII.
  - 3,000 missiles are to hit the US within the first hour.
  - Most industrial cities are to be destroyed.
  - Russian missiles placed in major US Lakes and Rivers (up to ten Nuclear Warheads/Missile); put there with American Government knowledge and approval.
  - To date, approximately 90% of the Conspiracy plan has been fulfilled on schedule.

*As an aside, this Helter Skelter could be exactly what Russ Dizdar is talking about (see chapter four on the Black Awakening).

Liberals in Congress and the talking heads in the liberal leftwing media that supports them want guns removed from society at all costs. People with guns can fight back. An armed society is a *safer* society, but it could become a militant society against a government that has run amok. We constantly hear the cry that guns kill people, complete with alligator tears from the politicians who really couldn't care less about their constituency. They are thinking only of *themselves* and the position they have in the government as a bureaucrat. They do not care that criminals have and will always be able to obtain guns and ammo. That really does not bother them. They can deal with and handle criminals. What is difficult for these individuals to handle is the average law-abiding citizen. Put a gun in the hand of the law-abiding citizen and that is cause for worry, where the liberal legislator is concerned.

At all costs, guns must be eliminated. It does not matter how many times these liberals are shown that removing guns from society will not make it safer. It does not matter what type of statistics they are provided with. They are deliberately deaf, dumb, and blind to these types of arguments because what they want and need to have is a society without weapons. That is their bottom line and they will use whatever excuse makes them sound as though they are truly concerned. They aim to create fear in the average citizen so that they will listen to and agree with the false rhetoric created by the leftwing politicians.

It is no different for politicians whose chief aim is fighting for women's rights. People like Ted Kennedy and others couldn't care less about a woman's right to choose. Being Pro-Abortion is simply good politics and it is what gets people elected and re-elected. Ted Kennedy spent years looking as though he wanted nothing more than to ensure that women continued to have the right to kill unborn babies. In reality, all he cared about was being re-elected. If abortion was not the hot button issue that would maintain his election status, he would certainly find the one that would.

Since the election of President Obama, it has become exceedingly clear that his goals are to help complete what has not yet been completed with respect to the Illuminati's plan. He wants guns outlawed just like every other liberal, but he knows he has to be very careful.

President Obama has made some big missteps that have forced him into the corner to some degree. Prior to the midterm elections of November (2010), it was clear he had no interest or intention of working *with* conservative Republicans. However, *after* the election, when the Republicans gained the majority in the House, it was just as obvious that he would be *forced* to work with them.

Let's be clear here, though, in recognizing that the Illuminati likely have key figures in both the Democrat and the Republican groups. Why would they simply do their best to control one without at least trying to control the other? They dare not leave anything up to chance.

It is interesting that for the past few years, we have continually heard rumblings of a coming fuel crisis. It seems clear that the media has had a hand in creating this crisis because it was not long ago when they seemed to be throwing dice to see if gas prices would top $3.00 and then $4.00. It was not long before $3.00 came and then went. How long before we see a solid $4.00 here in the United States? Only the Illuminati seem to know.

It is the same with food. Every time the news is turned on, or a newspaper or magazine opened, there are more dire predictions about food shortages. Certainly some are real, while others are simply there to produce greater fear. Just yesterday, there was another article about the fact that "cheap food" may be going the way of the dinosaur. Certainly, when comparing grocery prices of today with what we saw even six months ago, we see that prices have obviously begun to rise.

These types of things instill the fear necessary for the average person to look to the government to help, and the global elite counts on it. A society that lives in dread is much quicker to give up even more rights if only the government would deal with it and make it better.

There are too many people who simply do not see what is happening with respect to government control. We all know how obnoxious it has become to fly on an airplane anymore. The hassle of going through the frisking, the scanning, taking your shoes off, your belt, emptying your pockets, and everything else has made flying very troublesome. Yet, in spite of the new rules that the TSA has foisted upon the flying public, there are people who can still be heard saying, *"If it makes us safer in the air, then I'm all for the new rules!"* This is exactly what our government loves to hear. They want people who are no different than automatons. They want people to obey without question because it not only makes their job easier, but allows them to turn their attention the more important issues at hand, like living the life of a king, while the rest of us work to support them.

Do the Illuminati truly exist? Each person will decide that for themselves. Suffice it to say that *something* is controlling the way the media spins things and that same someone or something is controlling many aspects of society.

Years ago, I recall that after seeing another idiotic and sexist (toward men) commercial on TV, my father pointed out that it was a goal of the elite to portray men – normally white men – as morons, incapable of doing anything for themselves without the help of a woman.

The reality is that for years, following the genre of shows where father really did know best, men have been routinely presented on TV as idiots. If you really need something done, ask Mom. Commercials are notorious for this and continue the practice. Recently, I saw a commercial about a plug-in air-freshener. It worked when it sensed motion. Well, there was dear ol' dad trying his darndest to set the thing off by waving his hand in front of it. When that didn't work, he tried a bit of a dance. Finally, his wife walked up, briefly waved her hand in front of the unit and it worked, to the chagrin and confusion of the husband.

Commercials like these are common place. TV shows like this are also common place. Sitcoms are the worst because it offers a chance to laugh at Dad, who is seen trying his best, but his best is just never good enough. He's a buffoon, though he tries hard not to be.

The other thing that has become prevalent on TV is the show where kids rule. Nighttime dramas have one young person after another as the main characters. These kids not only know best, but know far more than their parents. While the mother may know more than the dad, it is clear that the kids are far more intelligent and can handle anything that comes their way.

Shows like "Everybody Loves Raymond" provide laughter at the expense of the husband or father. In the case of the Raymond show, the wife not only knows everything but spends half her time treating Raymond like a little boy. It is difficult to believe that a grown man could act that way.

The relationship between Raymond and his onscreen wife, Debra, seems more like a mother/son relationship (except for the fact that every once in a while, Debra allows them to enjoy marital relations). These types of shows are not only absurd, but certainly send the wrong message to people, and have been doing so for decades.

By now, all people realize that men are morons and women know everything. This is exactly what the global elite have planned because it turns everything inside out and upside down. It is one of the ways to undercut society and take what God designed and overthrow it.

The *Illuminati* – whether real or imagined – certainly exists to some degree and in some form in the world. As stated, something has been moving the world further away from God and that much closer to annihilation. Obviously, behind it all stands Satan, wielding as much power as he has to overcome God's preordained order.

Satan cannot do it alone because he is only one individual. He has worked hard for generations to coalesce his goals using fallen angels and fallen people to achieve those very goals. In order for Satan's plan to come to fruition, he must work through those that live in this dimension. Without these people, he would not be where he is today and this world would not look as it does.

Absolute Obscenity

Recently, I watched a documentary on the evolution of the pornographic industry. There were a number of things I was not aware of and that was probably due to the fact that I really took little notice of pornography as I grew up. Yes, as a young, virile teenage male, I was definitely interested in the opposite sex, but porn was something that was beyond the scope of my world simply because it was not something that we had around the house in the form of adult magazines, nor was the subject ever really discussed.

Watching this documentary gave me a panoramic view of the porn industry, how it started, and how it became what it is today. It's certainly not a pretty picture at all, and in fact, it tends to highlight to very seamy side of humanity.

The first real porn film not only became well known but went to new heights with obscenity charges brought against a number of people associated with the movie. In the end, only actor Harry Reems was charged with anything and actually stood trial and found guilty. He faced five years in prison, but when Jimmy Carter was elected shortly after that a federal judge overturned that conviction. In short, it became a First Amendment issue.

It is difficult to look back to that time period – 1972 – and get a picture of life then, without the porno that seems to exist everywhere in society today. Then, not only were more mainstream porn films not widely known, but the subject matter of *Deep Throat* had really never been explored in any film.

So *Deep Throat* burst onto the scene and it made over $600 million dollars after being made on a budget of $25,000. The more interesting thing about *Deep Throat* is really not the movie itself, or the subject matter. The far more interesting aspect of *Deep Throat* was actually the *doors* that it opened for other movies to enter into the thoroughfare of American life.

I do not honestly believe that actors Linda Lovelace, Harry Reems, director Gerard Damiano, or anyone else associated with *Deep Throat* truly understood the fully negative impact that movie would have on society and the doors of hell it would open. What I mean by that is simple: Satan loves the shadows. He is most comfortable there…for now. He exudes confidence when he can hide behind people or things.

When *Deep Throat* was made and released, the furor it caused became an issue of free speech and expression. The people involved with the movie believed that it expressed the things that a man and a woman should be allowed to do in the privacy of their own homes. In other words, the opinions about the movie by those who supported it were seen as *altruistic*. The unfortunate part, though, is that Satan will use any method at his disposal to deceive, and that is exactly what he did then by using *Deep Throat* as a vehicle to bring a great deal of harm to this world.

In essence, the flood gates were opened with *Deep Throat* and what was claimed to have been altruism became unadulterated smut, and what drove the creation and growth of the industry after that had everything to do with prurient interests and desires, but above all things, *money*.

Evil has many faces because it takes a lot of different faces to ensnare people at their weakest points. But ultimately, all evil has the same desire, and that is to simply ensnare. The commodity that does that the best is money.

Looking back we realize that regardless what the government tried to do, it is easy to see that they failed. The reason they failed was twofold:

- Hypocrisy
- Money

It was shortly after Nixon began assembling a team of people headed by Charles Keating to go after indecency found in porn movies – and specifically *Deep Throat*, since that was the most well-known movie at the time – that Nixon was forced out of office. Having been involved in the Watergate Affair (with, interestingly enough, a source to Woodward and Bernstein named "Deep Throat"), it was clear to the nation that Nixon had been involved in spurious and even illegal activity. This was probably not new to politics, however Nixon was caught.

With Nixon forced out and the presidential elections not that far away, Jimmy Carter seemed a shoe-in simply because people wanted a real change. They certainly got one with Carter, who may wind up tying with President Obama as the worst president in recent history.

Once Carter was in and a federal judge overturned Harry Reems' conviction, things seemed as though it would level off. The problem though is that about this same time, video players were now available to the buying public. This meant that people did not have to go to theaters to watch movies...porn or regular. The porn industry took notice of this new technology. They also noticed that video cameras had become far less expensive. Now, the average individual could buy a camera. Moreover, the average individual could now make their own movie.

It was then that the floodgates really opened up and porn became so available that anyone who wanted to watch a porn movie could do so. It did not matter that the porn that was being produced was simply one sex act after another. The focus became sex for the sake of sex.

What the average person does not realize is that every time some new phenomenon takes center stage that had been previously held in check, it seems to overflow into society *unchecked*. This is exactly what happened with pornography.

If we consider the state and level of porn in our society today, what sane person would argue that porn has not affected us? It seems clear that no stone has been left unturned where pornography is concerned. In many ways, it has become very much part of the mainstream. Consider the type of ads that are routinely on display in a magazine, or on TV, or in a newspaper. There are so many that have some undercurrent of sexuality to them that it is not only easy to lose count of how many ads there are like that, but it has also caused society to become both enamored with and unable to see the potent sexual images that continually bombard us on a daily basis.

All of this seems to occur beyond the scope of our awareness. It affects our subconscious, and because of that it has become far more dangerous than a porn film like *Deep Throat*. Don't misunderstand. No porn film has any redeeming qualities to it. However, there is not much hidden within porn movies or pornographic material. It is all right out in the open and affects our conscious awareness, while opening other doors to things of even more prurient interest.

In today's world, though Satan worked very hard to create *Deep Throat* and then worked even harder to use our government and the feminist movement to bring tremendous national attention, having succeeded there, he has now made porn much more insidious. Now, a good deal of porn affects people on the *subconscious* level. Most are not even aware of what they are seeing or hearing.

Compare this to computer technology. My 20-year old son has difficulty accepting the fact that personal computers were not really available on a large scale until the mid-70s. He never saw the transition from nothing to what we have today. When I was growing up, I played outside with my friends. We used our imaginations and played all sorts of games and had all sorts of imaginary adventures. One of my favorite pastimes as a youngster was dressing up like Batman or Robin and fighting imaginary villains with my friends.

At times, we would play football or create games in the lawn by raking paths through leaves. If nothing else, we would get on our bikes and simply ride around, being physically active in our world. I look back and that and then I consider the young people of today. They had none of that, and because of that it is no wonder that our students cannot read and write. They have no imaginations because they never had to exercise them.

Video games are so realistic, it is absolutely incredible. The 3-D graphics can make your head spin and they continue to improve with each new video system or game produced.

I try telling my son that when I grew up, a black and white television was the norm. Only rich people had color TV sets. While he mentally understands that, he cannot *fathom* it. How could there be a world without color TV? Sometimes I will invite him to watch an old movie with me that I grew up watching and he has a difficult time with it because it is not in color. That is like being raised in a society where all visual technology is in 3-D, but having to go back and view things in 2-D. Who would want that?

The point is that what developed throughout my generation already existed with his. This is the same problem with pornography and obscenity. It developed over time to what it is now. Unfortunately, too many today are not aware that it *has* developed from something else. Today, it is no holds barred and nothing is left to the imagination.

What was once verboten in mainstream movies has wormed its way into that venue. There is very little left for the mind to fill in in too many movies today. I read recently that the FCC is going to relax its standards for television since the networks believe they are in constant competition with HBO, Showtime, and other premium pay channels that can show far more than television is able to show.

In our modern day, the movie *Deep Throat* opened the door. In so doing, it not only cheapened the gift that God gave to a married couple for their enjoyment as well as procreation, but it has become very much like an overflowing sewer that has broken through or overflowed its walls. It seems as though everything has made its way into society.

All of this has served to erode God-given morals. When society has become so awash with filth that it does not even notice it anymore, something is terribly wrong. Of course, authentic Christians know that this is part of Satan's plan to overcome and conquer the globe. People with high moral standards become an issue for him and his insidious plans to recreate Sodom and Gomorrah throughout the world. Moral people become like Lot, who spent his days being vexed in his spirit for what he saw in the city he lived. It is obvious that Lot tried to restrain the denizens of Sodom, because when the angels came to him and the men from the city came out with rape on their minds, Lot tried to stop them.

Lot first offered his daughters – a poor choice, but in Lot's mind, had the perverted men of the city raped his daughters, it would have been better than raping angels. It is also clear that the angels had a masculine appearance. The point though is that as Lot tried to steer the men of the city away from doing what they intended to do, they verbally attacked Lot for his judgmental attitude towards them. They then promised to do worse to him than they would have done to the angels in Lot's home. All of this is seen in Genesis 19.

Moral people in general do not serve Satan's purposes. However, a person who is simply moral and not a Christian can change with the times so that they are not as restrictive as they may have been previously.

Authentic Christians cannot really change their opinion about something if the opinion they have was originally adopted because it was based strongly on God's Word. God's morals do not change and neither should ours.

As I consider how times have changed since my youth, my mind is boggled. It seems incomprehensible that so much in life could have changed, and yet that is exactly what has happened. Gradually, over decades, general morality became amoral and then finally immoral, yet to the average person it seems not to have changed at all. This actually causes the Christian to stand out even further because our morals – based on God's Word – have not changed.

So far, in this book we have seen any number of things that exist today that all began as something else, or simply as a kernel of an idea. Over time, those ideas have germinated, giving rise to other ideas, with those ideas giving rise to newer, stronger, less moral ideas. What we have now is a cesspool of immorality masquerading as morality, truth, and freedom.

The unfortunate part of all of this is that what people actually end up with is the furthest thing from freedom. They become increasingly enslaved to the very things they believe will set them free.

Our world is sinking fast. It is spiraling seemingly out of control into the vortex of immorality created by Satan and his hordes. Humanity in general has become an unwitting accomplice, yet all will be held accountable by God for their actions.

Just this week, as this is being written, a principal of an elementary school was shot and killed by the janitor. According to some, the janitor was generally grumpy with some of the students and staff. Apparently, there had also been a disagreement between the janitor and the principal.

As I read the story on the Internet, there was a place below the article where people could post comments. A number of people indicated that their hearts went out to the family and that they would pray for them. One individual wrote in essence that people needed to get over their belief in a god that does not exist. He went onto say that people alone are responsible for their actions.

I would agree with the second comment, but that does not dismiss or mitigate God's existence. God can fully exist and people can be fully responsible for their actions. There is no contradiction there at all, as some apparently believe.

This world continues in the dark shadows of impending doom and judgment. There is no getting around that at all. In spite of the blatant changes in society that have taken place due largely to Satan's direct involvement and supervision (along with the fact that God has allowed these changes to occur), it remains that the Christian's job is not done. In fact, for as long as we have breath, our job of evangelizing the lost will not be done.

Christians can expect God's moral code that we own and live under to come under much more severe attack. The attacks will increasingly be out in the open as well. It also seems reasonable to conclude that people will hate us simply for what we represent. Our presence will remind them of their own shortcomings, inadequacies, and guilt. People who feel this way because of another person's moral code normally turn and attack that other person either verbally or physically, and sometimes both.

As time steadily moves toward the coming Tribulation, it seems easy to see that authentic Christians will stand out from the crowd in greater measure. Can it be any other way? The world will become worse and that alone will put the light of adversity on authentic Christians. We will be seen as Lot was seen, becoming the source of the world's guilty feelings because of their own fallen nature and immoral attitude and demeanor.

I have begun to notice it on a larger scale in my own life these days. Attacks come more frequently. They seem weird, even out of place, and I am willing to bet that the people who are reacting to people like me are not even aware of the reason they are acting the way they are acting.

Recently, I began asking God to heighten my awareness of how the enemy works in his realm. I certainly knew what I meant by that request, and in my mind I had a picture of the veil being drawn back, allowing me a glimpse behind the curtain so I could actually see the powers of darkness at work, much the way Elijah prayed for that young man so that the young man saw for the briefest of moments the hills in the spiritual realm covered with God's warriors and angelic hosts (cf. 2 Kings 6). It appears though that God instead has chosen to help me see that attacks and confusing behavior by various individuals, while perpetrated by Satan's minions, are done *through* human beings. Paul tells us that our battle is not against flesh and blood (cf. Ephesians 6), yet that is often the vehicle Satan chooses to use in his attacks on authentic Christians. So does God want me to focus on people? No, but He seems to want me to realize that the vehicle of a person appears to be one of Satan's favored methods of attacking God's children. It is easy to forget that the person is the willing vehicle. Yes, they are culpable because they cooperated, but ultimately, the attack originates with Satan, not them.

I do not believe that Satan cares what he uses to bring his evil intentions to an unwitting society. In the end, he will use all at his disposal to bring about his own plans to unleash immeasurable evil on this planet. That evil must be released in increments, yet there is a time coming when there will be enough evil in the world that the entire dam that has held it back will simply be unable to hold back anymore evil. It will then give way to the flood of evil that empties from hell itself. That will be a very dark day indeed.

Back to Egypt

A few weeks ago (at the time of this writing), Egypt exploded in unrest. Turmoil arose due to the frustration over Mubarak's leadership and administration. Too many Egyptians have long felt that they do not have an adequate piece of the pie. Their anger became physical, with rioting, protesting, arrests, injuries, and even deaths.

The fact that we are in the end times says a great deal, and it is seen in these types of situations. Isaiah the prophet spoke about Egypt specifically centuries ago and his words – from the Lord – are recorded for us in Isaiah 19. It is there we not only see the transitional phases of Egypt's government, but we see the final outcome of Egypt's people and how they react toward the Lord of Hosts. What is good news is that in the end, it appears as though the nation itself becomes a nation that pleases God; a nation that knows who the only true God is and understands His love for them.

This is the future, but what is occurring now is something that seems to be described for us within the text of Isaiah 19. Upheaval due directly to the Lord's wrath, which pits Egyptian against Egyptian, is what is on display right now in Egypt.

"And I will set the Egyptians against the Egyptians: and they shall fight every one against his brother, and every one against his neighbour; city against city, and kingdom against kingdom," (Isaiah 19:2).

Because of Egypt's idolatry (v. 3), the Lord promises to hand them over to a cruel master. Verse 4 tells us this very thing.

"And the Egyptians will I give over into the hand of a cruel lord; and a fierce king shall rule over them, saith the Lord, the LORD of hosts."

With all of the fighting, protesting, and violence that is now occurring in Egypt, obviously something needs to break wide open. The Muslim Brotherhood waits in the wings and certainly wants to be part of any government that comes to power. If the Muslim Brotherhood gains a foothold in the new government, the government they will want is an Islamic government, not a secular government as many in Egypt today want. In fact, this is what they are fighting for now. They want a much more democratic government than the one that Mubarak has given them.

The Islamic groups like Muslim Brotherhood want to turn the country toward a strict or radical Islam. This is the type of Islam where Sharia is the law of the land and in spite of the false rhetoric that radical Muslims and clerics try to pawn off on the world, the reality is that Sharia shows no mercy and in general treats people as things, not human beings. It is a throwback to the days of an eye for an eye and tooth for a tooth. It is the type of law that the Pharisees wanted to use at every turn. This is why they were quick to pick up stones to kill a woman caught in the very act of adultery (cf. John 8 and also Leviticus 20:10). This type of law stems from a judgmental and legalistic heart and is not acquainted with mercy or compassion. In general, Sharia has no capacity for compassion because that is not what it is built upon.

This is the law that Muslim Brotherhood and others like them want to see in place in Egypt. If they get what they want, their representative from within their ranks will become the "cruel lord" over Egypt.

It appears that many in today's world prefer to deny anything negative about Islam or Muslims in general. The liberal plays well into this area, siphoning off any truthful information as if it came from the mind of some conservative "hatemonger" with nothing better to do than create hatred toward innocent Muslims throughout the world.

We know that many Muslims teach that Islam is a religion of peace. However, when we research this statement, we learn that Islam is a religion of peace only when all things are said and done. In other words, one of the strong beliefs within Islam is that in the end, Islam will be the only religion throughout the world. Because of this, there will be enforced peace. It will not be the type of peace that allows people of different cultures to live next to one another without arguing. This peace is not the result of two or three nations sitting down at the bargaining table and arriving at a peaceful solution to their differences.

The peace that the Muslim refers to is the peace that is foisted upon people by the final Islamic leader. Those who convert to Islam (if they are not already a Muslim) will be allowed to live. Those who do not convert will be executed. It is really that simple. So on one hand, Muslims are not lying when they say that Islam is a religion of peace.

On the other hand, it is clear that their definition of peace is not the same definition that the world routinely uses. That difference is stark, and it is one that will continue to deceive because of the very nature of the definition and the fact that Muslims feel no reason to fully explain what they mean by the word "peace."

The world is presented with a view of Islam that appears to want peace and seems to be working toward peace. The truth of the matter, though, is found in what Muslims – both moderate and radical – believe in their heart of hearts and teach to one another in secret.

I know of a woman who lives in Australia who spent two years undercover, essentially as a Muslim convert. She dressed in Hijab and Abbayah, gathering what she could to help prevent the formation of these dangerous groups in the area in which she lived.

She mixed daily with average Muslims – mostly women, or men in large mixed groups. It isn't possible to be cloistered in rooms with men unless there is an Imam or someone of authority there at the same time.

She tells me that contrary to popular belief, the average Muslim on the street is fully in support of terrorism. It is preached in the mosques that all those under the covering of Islam must breed the rest of us out of existence. It is interesting to note that wherever Muslims relocate to, they quickly begin to grow their own population from within, and in short order have what they consider to be their own Islamic village. Because of this, they begin overseeing their own daily lives with Sharia. In some cases, the police and other law enforcement officials stay completely away from these areas, not wishing to get involved.

Anyone who is not Muslim is truly the infidel, and though they may smile at us and sympathize with the losses due to suicide bombers, explosions from planes and what have you, they are quietly pleased as death tolls rise.

This same woman tells me that she has been in a myriad of religious gatherings and Eid or Bayram celebrations and has listened to the propaganda. Every single Muslim is required to support the move to eventually take over the world, creating a society over which Sharia is the law. This is all irrespective of how peaceful or seemingly friendly they may be in public.

There aren't many people who are aware of this, and this woman often listens with frustration as people say ignorant things, such as, "the Qur'an doesn't preach terrorism," or "it's not all Muslims, only the extremists." She points out that from her experience alone, it is all Muslims, and the Qur'an *does* preach terrorism.

The tragic truth is that while some governments (city, state, or national) seem to be unaware of what is actually happening, at least some in government seem to be in collusion with the purposes and goals of radical Muslims.

A recent article states that *"Israeli author and expert on the Middle East [Avi Lipkin] is warning Americans that Islamic immigrants could possibly flood the U.S. as a result of the events taking place in Egypt."*[18] Unfortunately, due to our own administration seated comfortably in the White House, these immigrants would be looked upon as heroes, not problems. This same administration currently looks the other way with respect to the continual flow of illegal aliens from Mexico, refusing to acknowledge the fact that many of these individuals are criminals from Mexico.

The same article informs us that *"Israel National News recently reported that the Obama administration has decided to allow Islamic professor Tariq Ramadan to enter the United States. Ramadan, an*

---

[18] http://www.onenewsnow.com/Culture/Default.aspx?id=1288670

Egyptian who currently lives in Switzerland, is a leading member of Europe's Muslim Brotherhood branch and is the grandson of the movement's founder. He was invited to teach at the University of Notre Dame in 2004, but the Bush administration revoked his visa because of donations he made to a blacklisted charity.

"However, the Obama administration has now decided to lift the ban and possibly allow Ramadan and Adam Habib, another Muslim professor, onto U.S. soil."[19]

One must ask why President Obama would even consider revoking the ban. Has Tariq Ramadan changed his tune? Is he now calling radical Islam evil? The problem will simply be exacerbated when/if the Obama Administration gets its wish and finds a way to grant blanket amnesty to the millions of illegal aliens already in this country. As the article points out, once this occurs, how could this same administration refuse to grant amnesty to these Muslims from war-torn countries, who have escaped to America for asylum?

One way or another, Islam is making tremendous inroads into the fabric of many cultures, including that of the United States. Muslims are determined to overcome non-Islamic nations through every legal means possible and if that does not work, terrorism in the form of suicide bombers and other violent means is always a card they are willing to play. Their very ideology depends upon it. The more they are able to conquer, the sooner their Final Mahdi can appear, bringing Islamic justice to the world.

---

[19] http://www.onenewsnow.com/Culture/Default.aspx?id=1288670

14

Superstorms!

It is certainly no secret that the weather has changed. Flooding, snowstorms, tornadoes, hurricanes, volcanic eruptions, and more have become the norm. These are not normal storms though. They are what scientists refer to as *Superstorms,* and many scientists believe they exist because there has been "*an unstoppable magnetic pole shift that has sped up and is causing life-threatening havoc with the world's weather.*"[20]

The quoted article goes on to say, "*Forget about global warming— man-made or natural—what drives planetary weather patterns is the

---

[20] http://www.salem-news.com/articles/february042011/global-superstorms-ta.php

climate and what drives the climate is the sun's magnetosphere and its electromagnetic interaction with a planet's own magnetic field.

"When the field shifts, when it fluctuates, when it goes into flux and begins to become unstable anything can happen. And what normally happens is that all hell breaks loose.

"Magnetic polar shifts have occurred many times in Earth's history. It's happening again now to every planet in the solar system including Earth.

"The magnetic field drives weather to a significant degree and when that field starts migrating Superstorms start erupting."[21]

This is exactly what we are experiencing across the globe right now. No sooner has Queensland Australia done being hammered with flooding when the Cyclone Yasi pounded the same area. Yasi was classified as a Category 5 storm, yet because the winds were far stronger, it should rightly be categorized as a Category 6.

The earth is surrounded by a magnetic field, which apparently has some now noticeable cracks in it, according to NASA. If this continues, there is nothing that would prohibit the field from breaking up and disappearing altogether. What would happen then? Such a major change in the earth's magnetic field would result in more Superstorms that would impact earth in a way that is not really imaginable.

If rescue workers – according to the article quoted – are referring to Queensland Australia as a war zone after Cyclone Yasi, one can only imagine huge portions of the globe being hit with superstorm after superstorm. The impact and collateral damage is what is described in the book of Revelation, chapters 6 through 18. Here in these chapters, John sees the events of the coming Tribulation/Great Tribulation unfolding, and it is not pretty. Huge mountains falling from the sky turn

---

[21] http://www.salem-news.com/articles/february042011/global-superstorms-ta.php

1/3 of the world's oceans into blood, not only killing life in the sea, but capsizing 1/3 of the ocean-going vessels that happen to be in the way of a huge tsunami that is created from this falling, massive object.

Other objects falling from the sky destroy 1/3 of the fresh water, and in other areas crops fail, causing pestilence (sickness) and death to people and animals. The tribulation is not going to be pretty. The only good thing about the tribulation is the multitude of people who are martyred because of their faith in Jesus. Many of these people prior to the start of the tribulation knew of Jesus and possibly even attended church. It will be after the start of the tribulation that these people will look at themselves and realize that they were living a lie, thinking themselves to be saved when they were not. By God's grace, they will come to see *and embrace* the truth about Jesus, thereby becoming members of His household.

This author was not aware of the fact that apparently, the earth has a "wobble" to it during rotation. This wobble – called The Chandler wobble – affects the earth and the way the poles move. *"The effect causes the Earth's poles to move in an irregular circle of 3 to 15 meters in diameter in an oscillation. The Earth's Wobble has a 7-year cycle which produces two extremes, a small spiraling wobble circle and a large spiraling wobble circle, about 3.5 years apart."*[22] If this wobble disappears, it is obvious that tremendous changes to the earth's poles will occur.

What too many people do not realize is that evolution is credited with creating everything. The problem is that there is way too much information, down to the minutest detail, that could not have simply occurred, but gives evidence of a prime mover or intelligent designer. This designer – in order to make everything work as it does – must have such supreme knowledge to know the intricacies of all things, that to credit life on this planet as stemming from something as vapid

---

[22] http://www.salem-news.com/articles/february042011/global-superstorms-ta.php

as evolution simplifies life's processes to such a degree that it becomes unbelievable.

Everything works in tandem. Everything is interconnected, but there must be something that holds all things together and causes them to work the way they work. That something is not some spurious working hypothesis that allows people to place their beliefs in how life began without having to credit the Author of Life.

The Bible tells us straight up that Jesus created all things and holds all things together (cf. Colossians 1). It is not only beyond the pale, but absolutely asinine to believe that all the intricate aspects of life could have happened by chance, yet as Paul tells us in Romans 1:19-23, *"Because that which may be known of God is manifest in them; for God hath shewed it unto them.*

"For the invisible things of him from the creation of the world are clearly seen, being understood by the things that are made, even his eternal power and Godhead; so that they are without excuse:

"Because that, when they knew God, they glorified him not as God, neither were thankful; but became vain in their imaginations, and their foolish heart was darkened.

"Professing themselves to be wise, they became fools,

"And changed the glory of the uncorruptible God into an image made like to corruptible man, and to birds, and fourfooted beasts, and creeping things."

The absolute reality is that people *prefer* and choose to disbelieve that God created, wanting instead to grab onto something that removes God from the picture. Paul tells us that proof of Creation is found in what has been created. Notice that Paul also says that though people know this, they chose to dishonor Him by crediting some ridiculous working hypothesis that has become the religion of science, called evolution.

You have to appreciate the fact that Paul also includes the statement *professing themselves wise, they became fools*. To a Christian, the idea of all of life simply happening by chance is so far removed from reality that it has no bearing in truth at all. Yet for those who insist that God does not exist, therefore could not have created anything, the same working hypothesis has become truth because their minds have become darkened. The result is that what is absolutely preposterous appears completely logical to these people.

There are some things that Satan does not even have to deal with in order for them to occur. The entire Creation has over it the curse that God placed on it in Genesis 3, just after Eve and Adam disobeyed God. This curse will not be removed until the physical return of Jesus. For now, because of this curse, the earth as well as all that inhabit it – animals and humans – are subject to the laws of entropy and other scientific laws that tell us that things left by themselves go from order to disorder; from good to bad, and from bad to worse. This is now the natural aspect of how the universe reacts because of the curse. This is why people and animals age. This is why death waits at the end of each life. This is why our bodies will one day give out no matter how well we take care of them now.

The weather is simply doing what it does as a response to the laws of entropy that were put into effect after the fall of humanity. Those scientific laws are actually laws that provide a limit to our lives and that is a good thing. Had God not put these laws into effect, and had He not chased Eve and Adam out of the Garden of Eden before they were able to eat from the Tree of Life, people would live forever in physical bodies, but all the while becoming worse and worse.

Death provides the remedy for our physical bodies now. It allows us to fly free from what Paul calls this tent (cf. 2 Corinthians 5:1). Without death, we would be forever encased in a body from which we could not be free.

It is amazing how people see things, yet see nothing. All around us the weather is doing things that we have really never experienced. Yet people continue to see it (if they notice it at all) as an anomaly, not something that is becoming the norm.

People continue to live their lives – giving in marriage, being married, eating and drinking – while God is providing so many different and obvious notices that He is there and in control. Who is noticing? Just like the days of Noah and Lot, people went on with life irrespective of how bad things were around them. Today, people laugh at the idea that Noah existed except as one of the Bible's "tall tales." The same applies to Lot. Archaeology is proving the Bible to be correct and still people refuse to take note.

Superstorms are here and we will undoubtedly see more of them, if scientists are correct. They may well become the normal pattern of weather in the near future. If that happens, then people will simply get used to them and because of that, not lift an eye when another Superstorm hits someplace in the world. They will be seen as simply being part of another cycle of nature.

The problem is that even if these are cycles in nature, God is obviously using them to get our attention. We would do well to notice and listen.

15

Muslim Sends the Wrong Message

Muzzammil "Mo" Hassan of Buffalo, New York, is guilty of killing his wife, something he never denied. Ironically enough, Hassan and his wife – Aasiya Hassan – originally started their TV studio because they wanted to combat what they felt was a negative stereotype toward Muslims in general, which began shortly after the 9/11 attacks.

However, in 2009, Hassan killed his wife by stabbing her, and then did what radical Muslims seem to do best when they're not screaming their hatred-filled rhetoric: beheaded his wife. Hassan claimed that he was the victim of spousal abuse and police have stated that they had been called to the Hassan home previously but did not elaborate. Considering the fact that Hassan is over six feet tall with a stocky build and his wife was fairly slight of build, the idea that she could do any noticeable damage to him is very difficult to believe.

One of the prosecutors has stated that Hassan bought two hunting knives *"less than an hour before the attack, parked his luxury vehicle out of view at the [TV] station and then hid in wait inside. During a 37-second frenzy that began when Hassan's wife walked through the door, he stabbed her more than 40 times in the face, back and chest and decapitated her. Surveillance video captured some of the attack inside a darkened hallway."*[23]

When the killing was first discovered, the idea that this may have been what Muslims call an "honor killing" was downplayed by Hassan's attorneys. Honor killings occur when a male Muslim believes that either a wife or daughter (or some other female relative) has brought dishonor to their home by doing something as simple as being seen alone with another male. Of course, nothing happens to the single male that the woman was with, nor does anything happen to the Muslim man/men who carry out the honor killing.

Is there a motive that would prompt Hassan to undertake an "honor killing?" It appears as though Hassan had been served with divorce papers from his wife approximately a week before the murder took place.

Certainly, in Hassan's eyes, as a Pakistani-born Muslim, his wife seeking a divorce would be seen as something that would dishonor him as the head of the home. In radically Islamic countries, this is all that is needed for the husband to commit murder and call it an honor killing.

---

[23] http://www.onenewsnow.com/Legal/Default.aspx?id=1290650

Hassan, who was married previously and had two children from his recent marriage and two from his previous marriage, had gone through four lawyers, firing all of them except the fourth, but replacing that one with himself. The fourth lawyer was retained as an advisor.

It is ludicrous to believe that Hassan actually expects people to buy the complaint that he was the victim of domestic abuse. While it is possible, by and large, it is the man who is the perpetrator of domestic abuse. Certainly, when a man is larger than a woman, it makes the allegation even that much more difficult to believe.

In strictly Islamic countries, men literally get away with murder and there is little to nothing a woman can do about it. In fact, even in cases of rape, in order for a woman's accusation to be heard, there must have been four male witnesses. How ludicrous is that? So while a woman is being raped, at least four men must be standing there seeing it, and apparently it seems that the fact that they might not have done anything to help the woman does not enter into the judge's decision regarding the veracity of the woman's accusation. This is absurd, yet that is Islamic law. At the same time, radical Muslim men would have the world believe that women are treated with respect – all the while they remain hidden behind their Burka except for their eyes and hands. This is how women are respected, by making them invisible to society?

In truth, radical Muslim men continue to have seriously antiquated and even disrespectful views of women. They do not do what they do to honor them. They do what they do to protect themselves (the men) from being tempted by a woman. If they cannot see her figure, her face, or other parts of her that may cause sexual titillation, then they won't be tempted to rape the woman. It sounds like the men need more than a few lessons in self-control. But this is not how Muhammad himself lived. It is historical fact that Muhammad was enamored with very young girls. He "fell in love" with a six-year-old by the name of Aisha, though to his credit, he did not "marry" her until she turned nine. That was big of him.

In radical Islam, men are the ones who enjoy the privileges. Sadly, as more of these types of situations come to the fore, maybe more people will come to realize that truth about Islam and in spite of what many Muslims would have us believe, it appears that radical Islam is more of the norm, instead of the exception to the rule.

In one case, the mother of an eight-year-old bride who had been forced to marry a 58-year-old man filed for divorce, but the judge ruled against her saying she had no right to file for her daughter. He further indicated that the girl was the one who had to file for divorce and was not eligible to do that until she reached puberty.

While there are no minimum age requirements for marriage, the only requirement is that permission must be given for a young girl to marry someone.²⁴ These are tragedies and should not be allowed to occur, yet they do anyway simply because women are considered to be less than chattel. Young girls and women are put on this earth for the Muslim man, for his purposes, to use and abuse as he sees fit. Women in Islamic countries have virtually no rights at all.

According to the December 2010 issue of *National Geographic*, "*an estimated 2,300 women or girls attempt suicide each year. Many set themselves on fire as a way to escape domestic violence.*"²⁵ If they do not die from the attempt, they are severely disfigured for life. "*Bibi Aisha was 19 when...her husband beat her from the day she was married, at age 12. When he beat her so badly she thought she might die, she escaped to seek a neighbor's help. To punish her for leaving without his permission, her husband, who is a Taliban fighter, took her to a remote spot in the mountains. Several men held her while he cut off her nose, ears, and hair. She screamed – to no avail.*"²⁶

No Muslim man would deign to treat his animals as badly as he is allowed to treat his wife. It is a constant quandary for women in these Islamic countries because of their complete lack of rights. According to this same article in *National Geographic*, one "*female inmate at a Mazar-e Sharif prison [had] just been released, prompting Maida-Khal, 22, to cry out because she is still trapped in her cell. When Maida-Khal was 12, she was married to a man of about 70 who was paralyzed. 'I was so young, I couldn't carry him because he was so heavy, so his brothers would beat me,' she recalls. When she asked for a divorce four years ago, she was imprisoned. 'I am in jail because I don't have a* **mahram** *[male guardian]. I can't get a divorce, and I can't leave pris-*

---

[24] http://www.themuslimwoman.org/entry/young-brides-a-miserable-life-for-little-girls-in-saudi-arabia/
[25] National Geographic, December 2010, page 33
[26] Ibid, page 39

on without a man.' She says, with remarkable understatement, 'I have had a difficult life'."[27]

This is the type of lifestyle that radical Muslims want to foist on the entire world. Their rhetoric states that all people will be respected, even those who do not convert to Islam. Really? It is clear that they have no respect for women in general, yet the world is supposed to believe that this lack of respect is an anomaly and not the norm.

---

[27] National Geographic, December 2010, page 47

16

The Danger of Leaving Islam Unchecked

Are you Islamaphobic? Have you been accused of hating Muslims? Do you believe that Islam is a religion of peace? Are the ideologies of Islam and conservatism able to exist side-by-side? Today, it is becoming increasingly more prevalent to be labeled an "Islamaphobe" if you speak out against the ideology of Islam. No one likes to be called any word that ends in "phobe," and so at all costs, most people do everything to avoid that.

One of the tactics (among many) that radical Muslims use today within the United States and other democratic countries is to label people who speak out against them as *Islamophobes*. Since this is seen as being connected to hatred of someone or a group of people, it is designed to shut people up who oppose Islam.

The reality exists that more and more radical Muslims are pushing themselves and their beliefs on American society. Just recently, in a town where I spent a good portion of my life - Binghamton, NY – a conference was held by the UMC, or United Muslim Christian Forum. What they pushed publicly was peace. It was founded by El Sheikh Syed Mubarik Ali Shah Gilani, who is one of the Islamic leaders in Pakistan and who has at best a very questionable history of potential connections with terrorism, and at worst, is a terrorist himself. This group is affiliated with the M.O.A., Muslims of the Americas, a very anti-Semitic and extremist group within the borders of the United States.

The Muslims of the Americas has its headquarters in what they call "Islamberg," near Hancock, New York. In 2009, the Christian Action Network produced an undercover movie showing the amount and type of training that occurs there in a huge private compound.

One of the things that the public face of Islam here in the United States wants us to believe is that they – Muslims – are here to simply practice their religion and get along with others from a variety of faiths. In essence, Islam would like the world to believe that it exists based purely on peaceful motivations and intentions. If that is true, then we have questions to ask: why the terrorism? Why the suicide bombers? Why bother to fly planes into buildings, in which nearly 3,000 people were sacrificed to Allah?

In fact, why are there groups of Muslims in this country involved in combat training? What are they planning for and why are they planning it?

On one hand, what we hear and see on the public face of Islam here in the United States is from people who present Islam as peaceful.

They also state quite clearly that the Jews are the ones who have created all the problems and they are doing everything they can to bring about a revolutionary war that is meant to plunge the United States into war with Arab nations.

Many of these individuals teach at colleges and have written books on why the 9/11 terrorist attacks on the World Trade Center were really an inside job, perpetrated by Jews against the world. It seems that too many people are too willing to believe the lies that these individuals are stating.

If Islam is such a peaceful ideology, how can it be so misunderstood by a large percentage of Muslims throughout the world? The answer to that lies purely in the way Islam is understood by individual Muslims. There are essentially two branches of Muslims:

- *The Sunni*
- *The Shi'ite*

We might refer to these two groups as moderate or gentle for the Sunni, and radical or violent-prone for the Shi'ite. I will use the term moderate for the generally (though not always) gentler Sunni group and the term radical for the more violent Shi'ite group.

To have splits within religions or ideologies is not unusual. The Reformation brought about numerous splits from Roman Catholicism, which resulted in bloodshed and martyrdom. However, it can honestly be stated that the split that occurred within Islam between Sunni and Shi'ite Muslims is one that has probably caused the most bloodshed.

When Islam first began through Muhammad, he was very open to living peacefully with Jews and Christians. In fact, during the very early years, Muslims would pray toward Jerusalem daily. There are numerous passages in the Qur'an – Islam's holy book – that actually teach peaceful coexistence with Christians.

"And argue not with the people of Scriptures, unless it be in a way that is better. Say: We believe in that which hath been revealed unto us and revealed unto you; our God and your God is one, and unto Him we surrender" (Sura 29:46 from the Qur'an).

This type of belief was one of the motivating factors within Islam in the beginning. However, after a time, Muhammad began to gain more power where he was living (Medina), and because of this power, he realized he did not have to continue to try to be friendly toward the Jew and Christian because both of these groups refused to accept him as a legitimate prophet.

Other passages in the Qur'an began to reflect his growing hatred for those outside of Islam. Sura 9:5 directs Muslims to *"Slay the idolaters wherever you find them and take them captive and besiege them and prepare for them each ambush."* Verse 29 in the same Sura says, *"Fight against such as those who have been given the Scripture as believe not in Allah nor the Last Day."*

So just as we see that Islam underwent a major change since its inception, so also has a major split occurred within the ranks of Islam, creating two main groups of Muslims.

This split was created because of individuals who could not agree on who the next Islamic ruler – or Caliph – should be. After Muhammad's death, a third Caliph was chosen, but he was soon murdered.

Muhammad's own son-in-law by the name of Ali became the next Caliph under major opposition, including opposition by one of Muhammad's own wives. Ali was murdered five years after assuming power as Caliph.

The next individual to assume power as Caliph was Muawiya, who began the dynasty referred to as Umayyad Caliphate. At this point in time, the Shi'ite Muslims came to believe that the only person who should serve as Caliph was someone who was directly descended from Muhammad. The Sunni Muslims did not really care about that part of it.

Regarding these groups – the Sunni and the Shi'ite – both have a number of common beliefs:

1. Both believe that God is ONE – there is only one God
2. Both believe that Muhammad was the last prophet
3. Both believe that one day Allah will resurrect all human beings and question them – not judge them – regarding what they believed and how they lived their life
4. Both groups agree that the well-known sins like murder, adultery, stealing etc. are true sins
5. Both groups also agree on the Five Pillars of Islam
    a. The first, Shahadah, is a saying professing monotheism and accepting Muhammad as God's messenger
    b. The second, Salat, is the five daily Islamic prayers
    c. The third pillar is Sawm, which means fasting, and within Islam three types of fasts are recognized
    d. The fourth is Zakāt, and is the practice of charitable giving
    e. The fifth pillar of Islam is called Hajj, which is the required pilgrimage to Mecca that must occur once in the life of every Muslim during their holy month of Dhu al-Hijjah
6. There is also a sixth pillar, which has become well known throughout the world. It is called Jihad. Jihad – or holy war – is practiced by a growing percentage of Muslims throughout the world. Depending upon the individual Muslim, jihad can also refer to the great inner struggle against sin.

It is impossible to know what every individual Muslim means by the use of the term *jihad* and it is also clear that some Muslims do not recognize jihad as a legitimate pillar.

However, the fact that some Muslims not only recognize Jihad as a legitimate pillar of Islam but view it as something that must result in the deaths of non-Muslims is of great and growing concern. The difficult aspect of this is attempting to discern who is and who is not a radical Muslim.

For instance, Imam Rauf, who has been in the forefront in the attempts to build the mosque near Ground Zero, only a stone's throw from the destroyed World Trade Towers, claims to be a moderate. He would like the world to believe he is a Sunni Muslim, one of the gentle Muslims that truly do wish to live in peace with all other human beings.

However, the fact that we know the kinds of things he says when he is not in the United States, as well as his unwillingness to even consider moving the Ground Zero mosque to another area much further away from the demolished World Trade Center, speaks volumes. Since he is unwilling to recognize that over 70% of Americans would be thoroughly offended by the presence of this mosque in the shadow of the World Trade Center, it becomes clear that he not only has virtually no concern at all for those who were killed when radical Muslims slammed hijacked planes into the towers, but also has no concern or feeling for the people who lost loved ones in that brutally senseless act of murder.

So in spite of Imam Rauf's rhetoric about being a moderate Muslim, we can see from his demeanor and his words that he is not a moderate, but is in fact a radical Muslim simply fronting as a moderate.

Is it wrong to generate a judgment about someone based on what they do and/or say? Absolutely not. People do that with professing

Christians all the time, don't they? They see a person who is noted as being a leader within the Christian community and they expect him to act a certain way. When they read about this same man being arrested on charges of embezzlement, rape, or child molestation, they normally conclude that something is desperately wrong. Too many people wrongly conclude that this is simply another hypocrite Christian, though, when in point of fact, for a person to simply say he or she is a Christian, yet not live a life that mirrors that of Jesus, may well mean that they are something else than what they profess to be.

History is filled with examples of people who used Christianity or their religious beliefs to take advantage of people and make themselves rich. This does not mean that they are or were actual Christians. It means that they used something to their advantage so that they could get away with crimes, since they believed that their facade of Christianity or being religious would help them to continue to appear to be something they are not.

This is true of people from every walk of life. We tend to judge people's testimony or character based on their actions and words. Do their words and actions mirror their beliefs?

In the case of Imam Rauf, it quickly becomes clear that unless he is using a completely different definition of what it means to be a moderate Muslim, he is a radical Muslim in disguise.

But what do radical Muslims hope to achieve?

Radical Muslims look to the history of Islam and desperately want to regain what they had centuries ago when they ruled much of Europe from Spain.

The reason that radical Muslims do what they do has everything to do with the fact that they believe Muhammad when he said that all Muslims should fight against any who not only do not view Islam favorably, but who are not Islamic themselves.

All people who stand outside Islam are considered to be infidels, and the only options given to infidels are to convert to Islam or die. This stems from Muhammad's later teachings after both Christians and Jews rejected him as any type of authentic prophet.

I was watching another documentary the other day on al-Qaeda, Bin Laden, and the Taliban. One thing that Bin Laden said that he believes is the main difference between those of Islam and the people of the United States is that we love life, but Bin Laden and those who believe as he does love death.

To understand the mindset of these people, it is important to understand that they do not view life and death as most people do. Most people place a high value on life. Even as a Christian, I highly value the life I have with the God I worship, my wife, and my family.

I know that one day, I will die. I am prepared for it, but I do not necessarily wish that it would happen now. I believe that when I die, I will live with Jesus and all who have followed Him in this life. If you disagree with me, that is your right. I have no intention of killing people who disagree with my own religious beliefs. I doubt that you harbor that kind of resentment toward those who do not agree with you either.

This is the problem – the *main* problem – with radical Islam. They not only see it as their obligation to kill infidels – those outside of Islam – but they fully believe they will be rewarded by Allah for the murder of innocent individuals.

A short while ago in an airport in Russia a suicide bomber killed at least 35 people and injured nearly 200. Though no one has taken credit for the bombing, many Islamic Web sites were posted with praise to Allah for the attack. Russian authorities believe the attack occurred because the Muslims of Chechnya want their own Islamic country. This connects back to 1999 when Putin attacked that area to keep it from seceding from Russia.

Radical Muslims do not want to work within the law to accomplish their goals. However, many in the United States are doing just that in order to push their beliefs to the forefront. We have already noted the seemingly peaceful face of Islam in places like Binghamton, NY where activists gather with those from other religions in a pretentious effort to prove that they are peaceful.

The problem, though, is who these groups are affiliated with and why. On the surface, these groups appear to want peace at all costs. They certainly seem to be doing things that are construed as peaceful. At conferences like the one held in Binghamton, NY, they are saying things that make people believe they want peace.

Again, the problem is *who* they are affiliated *with*, because that is what tells the story.

If a person said he was a Christian, attended church, carried a Bible, memorized Bible verses and looked the part of a conservative, polite individual, it would be easy to see that person as a Christian. However, if it was discovered later that the individual was part of the KKK, the person's Christianity immediately comes into question.

The KKK is known for its racist policies and horrific acts they have perpetrated on African Americans in this country. No one with any semblance of intelligence would believe for a moment that a person who was intimately involved in the KKK would also be seen as a true Christian.

Years ago, David Duke – who at one point was a Grand Wizard of the Knights of KKK, went into politics. While he was successful in gaining a seat in the Louisiana House of Representatives, he was completely without success in his two bids to become president of the United States. Why? Because in spite of what he insisted about himself – that he was simply a racial realist – most believed that he was every bit a racist at that point as he was when he was the Grand Wizard of the Knights of KKK.

Something is unfolding here in America that requires people to wake up. In spite of the fact that moderate Muslims exist and simply want to live peaceably with their neighbor, there are too many radical Muslims who only say that this is their goal. Inwardly, they want to dominate. Behind the scenes, they are doing everything they can to promote Islam as a religion of peace, but the sad fact is that they are willing to kill to achieve that peace.

That is *not* a religion of peace!

But we must ask ourselves this very important question: why do proponents of Islam want so badly to achieve this dominance of all other cultures? What is so important about that?

The answer is extremely simple. In fact, it is something that most will simply shake their heads or snicker at.

Radical Islamists believe that once they have gained control of enough of the world, their efforts will allow the Final Mahdi to come to the earth. This Mahdi is believed to descend directly from Muhammad and when he reveals himself to the world, the following things will happen:

- He will fill the earth with justice, relieving it from its oppression
- He will rule for 7 or 9 years.
- This will take place sometime during the Last Days
- His name will be Muhammad
- His kunya (patronymic) will be Abul-Qasim

To sum this yup, this Final Mahdi will lead Muslims to a great victory against the Christian Romans (i.e. All the white Europeans including the Americans). This coming war is called Armageddon.

It will end with a great victory to Muslims against Romans after six years. Muslims will take over their capital, Rome (this can be any city).

In the seventh year, the Antichrist will appear and a greater war will start between Jews and Muslims, which will last 40 days and will end when Jesus returns and Muslims kill all Jews. All people will convert into Islam. **Peace will pervade the whole world.**

This is what Muslims believe and this is what they work toward. They fully believe that the coming Final Mahdi will bring war against all those who are *not* Muslims. Under the leadership of this Mahdi, Islam will win and then all people who remain alive will convert to Islam. Following this, it is said peace will exist on the entire world.

So when we hear radical Muslims talking about Islam being a religion of peace, *this* is the peace to which they are referring. Islam is a religion of peace only *after* it overcomes all Christians, Jews, and anyone else who is not Islamic. That is how peace will be achieved. That is their goal.

While many of us are asleep at the wheel, simply going through each of our days the same way we have always gone through them, radical Muslims are training in compounds within the borders of the United States. They are training for the coming war that they believe the Final Mahdi will lead them into in order that they will dispossess all who stand in the way of Islam.

17

Inside Islam

This is the story of one woman's infiltration of Islam, essentially undercover; not all that hard to do for a woman who is willing to wear a burka. Obviously, though we refer to her as "Baseema" throughout, her actual name has not been used, and some of the other details of her life are also hidden or changed in order to protect her identity. What she shares is true and should wake us up, if not fully frighten us.

While we are busy hearing one thing from the government and Muslim groups like CAIR and ACORN and still another thing from the media, it would appear that this particular individual spent a few years living the life of a dedicated Muslim woman within the Islamic community and the story was altogether different for her from the one that is normally presented to the world about Islam. Is this merely a coincidence, or is what we are being fed the lie?

I took the time to ask her some pertinent questions about how she became involved with Islam and what it was like to be part of that community.

Baseema's story begins in her own area of employment in her native New Zealand. She noticed that since she had become part of a type of security work force, many Muslim men had also applied for and received positions in that same line of work.

"Watching these Muslims work, it became easy to understand why they chose to enter the realm of public security as their preferred employment. There were often comments from non-Muslims regarding the work ethic, or lack thereof of these Muslims.

"They were thuggish control freaks, and the more we got to know them, the more we realized that the oft-presented 'softened' public face of Islam was a lie. The realization that, in general, they didn't seem to be as intelligent as the average non-Muslim piqued my curiosity. It seemed impossible to have an intelligent conversation with more than a couple of them.

"I had overheard some pretty alarming conversations between them about groups of jihadists etc., when a job opening came up in a Muslim company. It was pretty amazing the way the timing fell into place. I applied for, was offered, and took the job. After a short time, I realized they were very close-mouthed in front of us - the infidels - and they were also very abusive, so I attempted an experiment at a Muslim shopping center. I wrapped a scarf around my head and draped baggy clothes on and discovered a whole different world. They were completely different. They spoke freely in front of me. I discussed this with

a friend in the police force and he suggested sharing it with a member of the federal police. I was asked then if I'd be willing to pass on any information I gathered. Agreeing, I moved into a house owned by Muslims in a Muslim community a long way from where I lived, began wearing the hijab[28] and put out that I was a new convert looking for friends."

For Baseema, essentially dropping out like that caused a number of hardships. *"I did lose a dear friend, who never understood why I suddenly disappeared, and I couldn't discuss with her what I was doing because it was too risky. That was sad, but I did think she would forgive me and was surprised when she didn't. My Christian faith remained completely untouched. God was with me everywhere I went, and I believe He kept me safe."*

Living in that world certainly has its risks, as it did for Baseema. The interesting thing though is that for those who *appear* to be genuinely interested in learning more about Islam and even willing to convert to that ideology, doors *will* open.

"The Muslim community in general is always excited to have converts. I was very convincing and struck up several very close friendships with people in the community. They were more than happy to involve me in their 'religion' and help me along the way."

Spending time within her new Muslim community provided Baseema with multiple opportunities to see what Muslim men, women, and families are like in reality. What might be hidden from public view comes into the open for those behind closed doors.

"The public face of Islam is totally different to the private reality. I was already amongst them when the [World Trade] towers were hit and even though I'm pretty jaded by the world and its machinations, I

---

[28] The hijab is the traditional head covering that while covering the head leaves the face uncovered.

found myself shocked by their behavior. In public, they sympathized and made moving speeches about the tragedy etc. In private they celebrated every time the death toll went up. They channel a great deal of money into their mosques, and the two mosques close to where I was were two of the very pro-terrorist ones."

All of this then leads to a question about how to receive Muslims. Do we receive their public face, or do we acknowledge that behind closed doors, there is a good possibility that they hate anyone who is not one of them? This certainly does *not* mean that we attack them – either verbally or physically. However, it *does* mean that we may need to constantly be on our guard because of the duplicity that may certainly exist within their community.

When asked how we should approach Muslims or react to them, Baseema stated, "*I would say to people, open your eyes. These people, who are so friendly and nice down at the local supermarket and fruit shops, fully intend to make Dhimmis[29] of you. The mission of Islam is to rule the world under a sharia society of government. It has nothing to do with whether they like you or not. Muslims are ruled completely by their religion.[30] The needs and wants of the average person are completely swallowed up by the edicts of the religion itself. It doesn't matter what they say to you, or how personable they are, or even how fair and intelligent some of them may seem. They will all bow under the plan of Mohammed, which is in actuality the plan of Satan. They will tell you their Allah is the same as God. This is a lie.*"

Yet at the same time, it is very difficult to get other people to believe that this is what Islam is and what Muslims believe. In dealing with Muslims, many of them may seem perfectly fine and amendable to different ideas. The truth though is that an orthodox Muslim cannot

---

[29] Dhimmis are Christians and Jews (and others) who do not embrace Islam, yet live under its rule. They in essence become slaves to Muslims.

[30] Islam, in the opinion of this author, is best seen as an *ideology*, which *incorporates* a religious mindset, but not solely a religion.

side with anyone outside of Islam. Though they purport to want to worship with people of all faiths, that is impossible for them, because they ultimately see Islam as being victorious over all faiths.

Regarding important people within Islam and Baseema's ability to have met some of them, it is clear from her own words that she was not ever able to meet someone who would have been truly important within Islam. *"I was not able to get close to 'important' people within the movement. Nobody does. This is why they keep the cells completely separate, so there is no link. It's all 'through someone, who is through someone else.' It is such a tangled web of connections that it takes many operatives with far greater resources than mine to break in. But, having said that, it is the information from people like me that gets those people in the door."*

Yet in many cases, it is not necessary to actually meet any higher-ups within Islam. Baseema shares with us the tone and tenor of meetings in which many Muslims interfaced. That tone obviously comes from the top down.

"I was in many meetings and rallies where the imams laughed about how stupid the general public is, and that it will be easy to take over the infidels because they are so concerned with political correctness that they are paving the way for their own defeat with pretty manners.

"The plan is to avoid the use of nuclear war if possible because they want the world for themselves. They say they have patience and they can wait to breed us out. The instructions given out at all the mosques and dersanes (preparatory educational course – usually having a large female contingent) is to have as many children as possible.

"The Muslim community all supports each other like a hive. They are able to breed these large families because they exist on the welfare systems of the countries they are in and are also supported by the more affluent members of the Muslim community. I personally knew of many

families of 4 to 6 children all living on welfare. The father usually sustains some kind of work injury, so in a lot of cases both parents are home. They are the large breeding families, and are often supported by others."

So we learn that: a) Muslims do not want to use nuclear bombs to destroy because they will be doing themselves more harm than good, and b) outbreeding the rest of the world is already at work in places like The Netherlands. They mean to outnumber the rest of the world one way or another.

Getting down to the roots of the matter, it is important to understand just what exactly motivates Muslims. What are their core beliefs where Islam is concerned?

"Islam is an ideology. The religious aspect is the bones of it, holding up the body of government. It is a very cruel, harsh and frightening ideology with very little of what we would call justice. It is based on the hard Bedouin code of existence, which is brutal and completely at odds with western society and utterly alien to Christianity.

"Mohammed was an egomaniac who married a much older woman who was comfortable financially. When she died, he used that money to support his lifestyle. The details of his many wives is sickening, right down to the marriage of a six year old girl who, the Muslims will proudly tell you, he didn't have sex with until she was nine. He did. It's a lie.

"Mohammed practiced "thighing"[31] with her as well as sodomizing her and molesting her from when she was six. The head of the Muslim religion and ideology was a pedophile. Pedophilia is practiced with small boys as the norm among Muslims, as they aren't allowed to touch the girls unless they can manage to get them as wives. This will all be allowable under a sharia law system."

---

[31] placing the male member between the thighs of a child

The world seems to want to ignore this, and the most fascinating thing is how many within the political system of the United States and elsewhere seem so eager to want to embrace Muslims and the Islamic community in general.

They seem to believe that things like *"thighing"* and other sexual practices on children are not the norm, and certainly no good Muslim would ever practice them. The truth though is that it seems equally as clear that Western society has little to no clue about the true inner workings of Islam.

It would appear that children are extremely important to Islam. We noted that the more children born into Islam, the greater the Islamic population becomes. Breeding them is extremely important. If what we hear about Muhammad – his propensity to enjoy young girls for sexual purposes –is indeed true, then this is the other reason children are important to Islam.

Commenting on this, Baseema states, *"As I explained earlier, I have heard the imams preaching that Muslims should have many children to slowly breed us out. Children are a means to an end in Islam. They are disposable, for the purposes of spreading the ideology like a cancer, for using as bombs – particularly the retarded or deformed ones. That is another issue.*

"Many of the children are born with congenital defects due to intermarrying, which they do to keep the family wealth close, and also so there aren't too many family dramas, which are a tendency among Muslims. They are a very aggressive and irrational group. Honor killings aren't thought of as such a shocking thing amongst them because of the disposability of children. Muslims, if you pay attention, are also doing their level best to worm their way into local, state and federal government positions. This is becoming relatively easy now because the voting population is growing large enough to outvote the infidel, which is anyone who is not Muslim."

Baseema continues with a warning filled with foreboding. *"Westerners, in general, have lulled themselves into a false sense of their own security. Their political correctness will bring them undone. In the anxious and earnest drive to be seen as 'civilized,' the western world is signing its own death warrant."*

The real tragedy should be obvious if what Baseema tells us is true, and there is certainly little to no reason to doubt it, based on the position of numerous Islamic countries such as Iran as well as the multitude of protests against Western society involving Muslims from all over the world.

When asked about the cultural outfit or dress of the women in Islamic communities and countries, Baseema is equally straightforward. *"The burka was instigated by the Bedouin because of the average male's propensity in that part of the world to breed with anything that moved. It began as a way to stop other men from attempting to breed with each other's property. That was centuries ago. It isn't much different today.*

"When the hijab (scarf) was outlawed in Turkish public and government buildings, many Turks moved out. The women I knew explained that it was their choice to wear it, which it is, but it's not really for any religious reason. It's more of an indication to the men that 'this is not a target, go rut somewhere else.'

"The more a woman is covered, the less chance that she will be used. In a sharia society, it is a safeguard, although not a very good one as scapegoats are always found. I felt safe inside the hijab and abbayah[32] *because the men left me alone the moment it was on. That explains the terrible rapes carried out on western women by Muslims. They really, really do not think they are doing anything wrong as to them western women are nothing more than 'prostitutes'."*

---

[32] The abbayah is the traditional robe worn by women in Islamic countries.

So much for the concept that Muslim men *honor* their women and it is for that reason alone that they want them covered. In truth, it seems that while it *can* be argued that a distorted sense of honor is part of it, the real reason for wanting their women covered is solely to keep other men away.

When asked what the reasons were for eventually leaving the Islamic community in which she had made her home for two years, she replied, "*I left after two years because I had gained as much information as I felt I could at the time.*

"*I gathered information about black-market firearms and cells. I also gathered information about general crime such as a car theft ring that operated between two cities and a large stolen goods ring. I gathered a lot of the general information I have shared here, as well as many names and contact places.*

"*The guns I witnessed and the people who were bringing them in were mostly from Sydney in NSW, so there is some smuggling coming in from there. There is a very large black market industry run by the Lebanese and Syrians up there. It is all tied up with the car thefts. The cars are stolen from Sydney and driven down to Melbourne, some of them with weapons inside, where they are hidden in the yards and garages of houses in the Muslim communities north of Melbourne. The guns are hidden inside the door trims and behind the radios and stereos in the cars. I have seen the guns pulled out from inside the dashes and consoles of the cars as well.*

"*There are a few Muslims who are 'panel beaters'*[33] *and car detailers who spray paint the cars and swap engines over. The house I stayed in actually had one of these men living there, and we had a lot of cars coming through.*

---

[33] A slang term referring to auto bodywork repair person

"To say much more about this would not be good. There are many Muslims in their communities who actually spend their time scanning papers and magazines and books purely with a view to finding any anti-Muslim sentiments. This is often how they will pick up on obscure documents and start their screaming attacks. It is usually the unemployed or those on pensions. They also have a few staff in their mosques that are given the task of seeking out discriminatory comments so they can all cry 'hard done by.'[34] They are a truly evil, insidious creeping disease."

This author has reported at least one incident at studygrowknowblog.com of a Muslim woman protesting her treatment by an Australian police officer. Fortunately for the officer, the entire incident was captured on his dash camera. Because of that, the officer was exonerated after the woman chose to bring her case to the public through the media. What she failed to realize was that her actions, demeanor, and accusations to the officer were all video-taped as it happened, prompting her to declare that she was not the person on the video and that someone else had made the claim, acting as if they were her.

The stupidity of this argument is seen for what it is, but had the incident not been recorded on the officer's dash cam, it is safe to say that it would have been her word against his. In that case, the entire Islamic world of Australia would have been up in arms until "justice" had been accomplished. Of course, it would have been Islamic justice, born of lies and hatred. That would not matter, though, because it would have furthered Islam's cause of being seen as discriminated against by the world at large.

Regarding the information that Baseema was able to learn during her two-year stint inside her Islamic community, it is clear that because of the danger involved, she has had to take steps to protect herself and her loved ones since she left that community.

---

[34] To feel treated unjustly/unfairly

"I have had no indication that any information about my activities in the Muslim community was known to them. I have changed my identity and location, and the federal police members I dealt with made sure I didn't feel I had been compromised. I was asked some time ago if I would be prepared to go back in. At the time I said no, but I have left that option open."

What always comes up in any discussion of Islam is the idea perpetrated by Muslims that Islam is a religion of peace. Baseema provided us with her insights into that as well.

"The attitude of the average politician is, as the Muslims predicted, ignorant. Many of those in government don't really want to know because that would mean taking action, which also might mean looking racist or discriminatory.

"The current political climate is a 'do nothing and try to look as good as possible' whilst doing that 'nothing.' The attitude of those in this part of the world in general is 'she'll be right mate' or 'it's none of our business, don't get involved.'

"To many Muslims, Islam is an ideology or religion of peace, because they believe that once the world is ruled by Islam, it will be peaceful. Their version of peace is, sadly, the western version of a horror story. It will involve all aspects of sharia law and terror for the average person. Death or subjugation for the majority of western women and an almost slave-like status for the men would be the norm."

It would seem then that too many politicians and leaders are simply hoping that Islam will go away or at least stay on their side of the fence. If Islam has anything to do with it, that will not happen. It is not an option for radical Muslims.

This may also be part of the problem for Western society. We generally break Muslims into two separate groups, and this author has done that as well. However, according to a growing body of evidence, this may in fact merely be cosmetic. In order to be a solid Muslim, the Islamic code must be believed and enforced.

There are times when Muslims are allowed to play along in order to pretend that they are willing followers of ideals outside of Islam, in spite of the fact that many of those ideas knock heads with the Islamic code. Baseema says as much when she notes, *"There is no such thing as a moderate Muslim. They just like to make you think they are."*

Should we listen to someone who spent two years within the Islamic community, or should we listen to those who are the public face of Islam? The question seems moot; the answer, obvious.

With respect to the Ground Zero mosque that proponents want built in the shadow of the WTC, we asked Baseema how she believes that endeavor would be seen by Muslims throughout the world if it is ever built. Would they see it as a victory?

"Yes. It will be seen as the western world capitulating completely. It will also step up the efforts of groups like CAIR. It will be the proverbial foot in the door."

Along these lines, we also posed the question concerning the way in which Muhammad pronounced victory in an area he had conquered. If history is any indication, it is clear that when he conquered a people from neighboring villages or communities, the first thing he did was to destroy churches and synagogues and rebuild in their place mosques for Islamic worshippers. Is this truly the way Muhammad did things or is that simply an inaccurate way of Westerners looking at a situation?

"It is believed that this is correct. If the world falls under a sharia society there will be no more churches or synagogues. None. There will be no Christians either, or Jews. The few that are left will have to go underground."

The future does not look good if people continue to turn a blind eye and a deaf ear to what is happening in the world today. Islam is most certainly on the rise throughout the world. They have in fact become emboldened by their gains, and that is pushing them onward.

It does not help at all that too many politicians are more blind than most because of a sense of political correctness. Whether or not Islam can be pushed back is certainly a question that deserves an answer and there are a number of groups attempting to do just that.

However, should these and all other efforts fail, people need to know what they will be up against. Imagine a world in which sharia is the law. It would force the world back to a day when Muhammad lived, when Bedouin tribes fought for control, when life meant little to nothing and there was great honor in fighting to the death for Allah.

What has changed from then to now is merely the modern technology associated with today's weaponry, as we have seen. It is far easier to kill thousands of people in one shot today than it was in the past.

People who are willing to unflinchingly look to the future to see what will become of civilization should Islam gain the upper hand are the same individuals who know that going underground will be the best way to survive. Those who refuse to acknowledge the true portent of Islam's increasing invasion and permeation throughout the world will be overtaken by it without sympathy.

It is always darkest before the dawn. Most would agree that things are getting very dark around the world. The one thing that is creating most of the darkness is the system of Islam.

Islam has been around since its founder, Muhammad, began it in the A.D. 600s. From humble and simple beginnings, a system grew from the spoken words of Muhammad that not only enraptures those who are part of it, but enslaves those who have no power because of it.

Islam is a growing force composed of radical idealists who believe that Islam *is* the mandated way of the future. They believe that Islam *will* achieve world dominance and when it does, the Final Mahdi will be revealed to the world. Once he is revealed, his reign will extend for 7 to 9 years and at the end of that time, the Antichrist will arrive on the scene in an attempt to overthrow him.

At that time also, according to Islamic teachings, Jesus will appear and fight with Islam and the Mahdi to kill all Jews. At that point, Muslims believe that peace will then prevail.

Why will peace prevail at this point? It will prevail simply because Islam will become the *enforced* ideology throughout the world. Any dissenters will be swiftly dealt with through execution.

So when Muslims tell the world that Islam is a religion of peace, what they mean by that is that in the end, peace will prevail because Islam will be the only game in town and Islam will be governed by Sharia law.

Based on all of this, it is important to realize that the world is not dealing with a few crackpots that can easily be either ignored or overcome. The world is dealing with a growing radicalism that believes in a jihadist mentality. That mentality states that Islam will prevail and nothing can stand in its way. This is what Islam teaches and it is what Muslims believe.

The time for ignorance is past. We must be aware of this approaching danger like we would prepare for a coming flood.

During the recent unrest in Egypt, with the general populace demanding Mubarak's ouster, the Muslim Brotherhood has been waiting in the wings. We can be assured that this Muslim Brotherhood was likely involved in some way with the civil unrest because they see their role as capturing Egypt for Allah. Once captured, Sharia law will be put in place as the governmental rule of law. This is what the Muslim Brotherhood hopes for and they work to this end.

We have also seen the unrest spread from Egypt to neighboring countries of Tunisia, Libya, Bahrain, and elsewhere. As this is being written, Libyan dictator Khadafy has been busy using force to put down the protests in his country. News reports indicate that at least 1,000 people have been killed, while Khadafy blames the uprising on Bin Laden and drug-tainted drinks.

Iranian President Ahmadinejad is now also on his high horse about the travesties perpetrated in Libya. This of course is in spite of Iran's own track record of civil unrest and force used to put down any protests. All of this unrest in the Middle East will simply provide more opportunities for Islam to become more active, grabbing power here and there while strengthening their hold on the Middle East.

The United States government continues to downplay or even deny that the Muslim Brotherhood has anything really to do with Islam. On February 10, 2011, *"Director of National Intelligence James Clapper called Egypt's branch of the Muslim Brotherhood movement 'largely secular'."*[35] This mentality flies in the face of all the information we have on the Muslim Brotherhood that tells an opposite story. People who do not know the truth may take Clapper's words as true because they do not know anything different. Those of us who know the truth realize that this is merely another attempt by the current Obama Administration to pull the wool over the eyes of the American people.

It is largely because of these ploys that many Americans have come to believe that President Obama is at the very least an Islamic *sympathizer*. With the number of books and resources currently available on the Muslim Brotherhood and its offshoots, it is patently ridiculous to believe that said Brotherhood is anything less than radically Islam-

---

[35] http://nation.foxnews.com/culture/2011/02/10/obamas-intel-chief-muslim-brotherhood-non-violent-secular-group

ic. Books like *The Muslim Mafia*, by P. Dave Gaubatz and Paul Sperry, or *Crimes Against Liberty*, by David Limbaugh, not only highlight the various connections that numerous groups like ACORN and CAIR hold with the Muslim Brotherhood, but also indict President Obama on numerous crimes such as a seeming abject hatred for the U.S. Constitution and a willingness to sidestep it at every opportunity.

To ignore the information in these and other books is to ignore truth, while naively believing that everything in the Oval Office is on the up and up.

As stated, President Obama is at the very least an Islamic sympathizer. He has shown this brand of favoritism since before being elected to the office of president, when he essentially stated that he was not opposed to sitting down with people like President Ahmadinejad to discuss some of the problems facing the world. If we have learned anything, we have learned that it is impossible to negotiate with terrorists, the likes of those from the Taliban, or al-Qaeda because they see life and death starkly different than most do.

For the Islamic terrorist, they believe they are glorified in death when taking not only their own life, but the lives of innocent people who are outside of Islam; people they refer to as *infidels*. Their goal is to rid the world of infidels, and to do so means to please Allah.

That is their core belief. Based on this, how does one approach an individual like this in order to communicate anything? Rational dialogue and discourse cannot be done, yet President Obama at least states that he believes it can be done. Either he is a complete idiot, or his words merely mask his true thoughts. This author does not believe Mr. Obama is an idiot.

The reality that must be faced throughout the world is that Islam has no intention of playing fairly or learning to work and live with people from other walks of life, cultures, or religions. The stated objective of

Islam is to destroy. If they are outside an area they wish to destroy, they will use all manner of force to achieve their stated objective. If they live *within* their target force is not necessarily on the table, though destroying the target politically is still the stated objective, and to that end they will work to destroy the target from within.

This fact is missed or ignored by many people today. They believe that since Muslims live in the United States and *appear* to be lawful individuals, they obviously wish us no harm. What these folks fail to realize is that simply living among us in the United States does not create within them a bond of loyalty to this country. Their loyalty is to Allah and him alone.

Their stated goal – to destroy – remains. What changes is *how* they will destroy their target. If we can gain any insight from groups like ACORN or CAIR, we know that at the very least these groups are tied in some form to the Muslim Brotherhood. If we investigate the Muslim Brotherhood, we do not have to go far to realize that not only is the Muslim Brotherhood *not* secular, but they are radically Islamic in ideology. This means that for them, Sharia law is the means to the end. It is how they come to control a society and maintain control.

Sharia law works on *fear*. It harkens back to the days of "an eye for an eye, a tooth for a tooth" mentality. If someone is caught stealing, the action taken is to lop of that person's hand. This not only punishes *them* for their crime, but teaches them (and others) that if they continue doing this, they will soon lose another hand.

If someone complains about the system of law, remove their tongue. If someone is caught in the act of adultery, stone them to death. If someone is found to be homosexual, execute them by hanging. It is interesting, though, that it is permissible for men to have sex with boys, but homosexuality is against sharia law.

The reality is that, as Baseema has shared, sharia law has no sense of decency or compassion built into it at all. It is harsh and brutal from start to finish and punitive to a fault.

People who extol the alleged virtues of sharia law do so because they are legalists who have gone to the nth degree in order to please Allah. They firmly believe that by keeping not the spirit of the law, but the *letter* of it, Allah will be supremely pleased. Why is this? It is because within Islam, in order to gain *salvation*, it must be earned. With systems such as Islam, with its built in Sharia law, the more legalistic, the better. Salvation is gained through the regimented efforts of all individuals to excel at keeping the law.

This is one reason why suicide bombers and other types of terrorists are honored within the culture. In essence, they are seen as giving up their lives while taking the lives of innocent people, and in so doing, they are immediately rewarded in the afterlife with 70 or so virgins.

Suicide bombers/terrorists are the extreme version of keeping Sharia law, and because of their "self-sacrifice" they receive the highest honor. When all is said and done, though, killing yourself along with other innocent people is merely self-serving. Since it is self-serving, it is selfish.

While the suicide bomber/terrorist believes that they are actually sacrificing for Allah, in truth they are sacrificing for *themselves* because of what they believe they will receive in the afterlife. Who among them would be so willing to die with others if there was no promise of the alleged rewards in the afterlife of 70 or so virgins?

Bin Laden is quoted as saying that the difference between Americans and radical Muslims is that those within the U.S. love life, while radical Muslims love death. To them, death is everything and this life is simply an opportunity to follow the letter of the written code in order please Allah. There is no real sense of having obtained or received salvation in this life, unless something as drastic as blowing yourself up while taking the lives of other people at the same time is part of the picture.

I believe Bin Laden is lying. If he thoroughly believed it he would himself become a suicide bomber, thereby entering the afterlife as a martyr for Allah. As it is, he spends all his time in *hiding* in order to stay alive one more day.

Bin Laden and others get their underlings and followers – those completely sold out emotionally to Allah – to do all the dirty work. They have no intention of lowering themselves to do the work of the Islamic automaton, who simply reacts or acts without thinking about consequences. There is too much at risk and too much left to chance for Bin Laden and other higher ups to put themselves in harm's way.

The world of Islam counts on the naiveté of people throughout the world, including many of those *within* Islam. They count on the global consciousness accepting their outward demeanor and verbiage as truth. They count on society either being unwilling or unable to see beyond the thin veneer of lies they have set up. Once the world begins to see what radical Islam is truly all about, things begin to fall apart for radical Muslims.

We can only hope that a growing population of the world will see more of the charade. Let us hope so.

Satan on the Rise

Throughout the world, things are in complete upheaval. Whether we are discussing *nature*, the *weather*, man's *inhumanity* to man or something else, things are obviously anything but peaceful.

In the opinion of this author – and it does not take a rocket scientist to figure this out – things will only get worse; *much* worse.

We are seeing and experiencing an increase in earthquakes and volatile weather conditions, creating what scientists call *Superstorms*. So far, we know that at least some of the world's major crops have been affected because of these weather conditions.

Russia's main export is wheat, which feeds much of the world. Due to crop failure, there is far less wheat available this year than last, yet the world's population continues to increase at an unsustainable rate.

Violence is on the rise and it is not just violence. It is violence that seems to have nothing to do with anything.

Not long ago, we saw the results of the tragedy in Arizona in which Jared Loughner killed a number of people and attempted to assassinate Congresswoman Giffords.

Also recently, we learned that Julie Schenecker, a 50-year-old mother of two, decided to kill her two children with a gun because, as she pointed out, they were "mouthy." This is unconscionable and more than that, it is *not* human. This is not how *human beings* act or react.

If we consider the amount of violent, irrational and deadly crime that occurs throughout the world on a daily basis, it could leave us scratching our heads and fearing for our lives.

We wonder when some whacked person might pull out a gun and decide something inside his head is telling him that he needs to kill people. This is NOT to say that guns should be outlawed. That solution is *no* solution.

It has become incumbent upon every person to be as aware as they possibly can be every day of their lives. We need to look around and notice our surroundings. The days of leaving our doors unlocked at home and in our cars is way past. It is not that we cannot trust anyone. It is that we cannot trust those whom we do not know, and *that* is a big difference.

In the Olivet Discourse, given by Jesus Himself and recorded for us in Matthew, Mark and Luke, Jesus outlined what would happen, not what *might* happen, but what *would* happen as time progressed toward the end of the age.

We note that the disciples asked several questions and understandably wanted to know when Jesus would return, when He would set up His Kingdom, and when this age that we now live in would come to an end. Jesus answered those questions clearly and succinctly. Some try to make it much more difficult than it has to be.

Some people argue that Jesus was talking about *His* generation – the generation that was alive during His time. That is impossible if we understand that the disciples wanted to know *when* the age they lived in was going to come to an *end*.

It is the *same* age that *we* are now living in. This age (which is the same age as when Jesus lived) has *not* ended yet. It *will* end when Jesus physically returns, and regardless of what Harold Camping says, Jesus will *not* be physically returning on May 21st. I cannot *wait* until that day comes and goes to hear what the excuse will be from Mr. Camping!

Jesus spoke about "this generation" and the fact that all the things He had just outlined would happen before the end of the age. He could *not* have been referring to the generation alive at the time because all of the things He highlighted have not come to pass, and most importantly, the *end of the age* has not occurred yet.

We know the *end will* occur when Jesus returns physically. People like to play allegory games with the Bible – a very dangerous game, because we are dealing with God's Word, not ours. Because of that, it is incumbent upon us to learn HIS meaning.

People argue that Jesus returned spiritually when Jerusalem was destroyed in A.D. 70. This is absolute garbage. Jesus will return physically and *every* eye will see Him do it! That is not a secret return that no one – not even authentic Christians – will be aware of.

Jesus spoke in the Olivet Discourse of His *physical* return. The idea that some have changed that to mean an invisible, spiritual return is nothing more than changing His Word, making Him a liar.

He will be back. When? I cannot give you a date. I *can* tell you that things are ramping up. We see weather going crazy, we see people going crazy, and we see the things that Jesus spoke of in the Olivet Discourse have come to pass.

It does not matter that people *want* peace. It does not matter that people think they can *believe* peace into existence. The only thing that matters is what God's Word says on the subject.

The facts and even the educated guesses that have been put forth in this book are in some cases too difficult for us to believe. However, they should give us reason to pause and consider. Is the Bible true? *Can* it be true? If so, what is in store?

The reality is that God has given us His game plan in the Bible. He has shown us what He is going to do. Every person has to make a decision. Is the Bible a worthy book to consider? Is it truthful? Will *you* believe it? Whether or not you believe it has absolutely *no* effect on the veracity of Scripture. Believing it or not only has an effect on *your* life.

Consider this. During the days of Noah, no one believed him. According to the Bible, it had not rained prior to the great flood. It appears that from Scripture, we learn that a thick cloud of moisture encircled the earth. That along with dew from the ground was what watered the earth every day.

So here is Noah building this huge Ark, and it is no wonder people laughed. They chose NOT to believe him. What happened? Well, if you believe that the global flood occurred as the Bible says it did, you know that everyone who was *not* in the Ark was killed. The fact that they did not believe Noah did not change the truth. It merely affected their lives.

If you can honestly say that the Bible is a crock and what we are experiencing are simply natural cycles, then you should hope with everything within you that you are correct. If you are wrong, your belief will have changed nothing except how the truth of the Bible affects *you* and *your* life.

Satan is on the rise, being allowed to do more of what he wants to do, yet it is all under the watchful eye of God Almighty. All of Satan's carefully laid plans will come to nothing, but first they will be used to bring great glory to God.

Satan is extremely powerful; however, he can do nothing without God's permission. He is bound by the limits that God has placed on him. Though a time is coming when Satan's power will seem to be limitless, the fact of the matter is that he is overseen by the Lord of Lords and King of Kings.

God is allowing Satan greater leeway to bring things to fruition that are foretold in Scripture. We have discussed a number of these things in this book. What does that ultimately mean for you? It means only one thing: *you must be born again*. That is the only fact that you need to be concerned with now – whether or not you are a child in God's Kingdom. If not, whether you think so or not, you are a child in the camp of the enemy, Satan.

You can easily change your status, but there is only one way in which that can be accomplished. You must reject the lies you now live under and come to the cross of Jesus. It was there, at Calvary, that Jesus' life and death culminated in the perfect atonement. He died and received God's wrath willingly in order that you and I would not have to be on the receiving end of it.

If you have gotten to this point in your life and you have not dealt with the question about Jesus, it is about time you do so. You need to stop what you are doing and realize a couple of things before you go through another minute in this life.

- **Sinner**: you need to realize that you are a sinner. You have sinned and you will continue to sin. Sin is breaking the laws that God has set up. We all sin. We have all broken God's laws and that breaks any connection we might have had with God. Sin pushes us away from Him.

    Romans 3:23 says *"For all have sinned, and come short of the glory of God."* That means you and that means me. All means all. That is the first step. We need to recognize and agree with God that yes, we are sinners. I'm a sinner. You are a sinner. This results in God's anger, what the Bible terms "wrath."

- **God's Wrath**: Romans 1:18 says, *"For the wrath of God is revealed from heaven against all ungodliness and unrighteousness of men, who suppress the truth in unrighteousness."*

    This is as much a fact as the truth that we are all sinners. Because we are sinners – by breaking God's law(s) – God has every right to be angry with us and ultimately destroy that which is sinful. If we choose to remain "in" our sinful states throughout this life, we will – unfortunately – be destroyed with the rest of sin.

    Fortunately, there *is* a remedy, and it is salvation.

- **God's Gift**: In the sixteenth chapter of Acts, a jailer asks Paul this famous question: *what must I do to be saved?* The question was asked because Paul and Barnabas had been imprisoned, and while there they began singing praises to God.

God then sent a powerful earthquake that opened the doors to all the prison cells, yet no one escaped. When the jailer arrived, he saw that everyone was still in their cells and after seeing that miracle (what prisoner would not want to escape from prison?), turned and asked what he must do to be saved. He was speaking of the spiritual aspect of things. He wanted to know how he could be guaranteed eternal life.

The answer Paul gave the man was *"Believe on the Lord Jesus Christ, and thou shalt be saved, and thy house"* (Acts 16:31).

This is not head knowledge or intellectual assent. This is *believing from the heart*. In fact, Paul makes a very similar statement in another book he wrote, Romans. He says, *"That if thou shalt confess with thy mouth the Lord Jesus, and shalt believe in thine heart that God hath raised him from the dead, thou shalt be saved. For with the heart man believeth unto righteousness; and with the mouth confession is made unto salvation"* (Romans 10:9-10).

When we fully believe something, we confess that it is true. It must begin in the heart because that is where the will is located. We must want to believe. We must endeavor to believe. We must seek to believe.

We must stop giving ourselves all the reasons to deny or ignore Jesus. As God, He became a Man, born of a virgin. He clothed Himself with humanity that He might show us how to live and in so doing, would keep every portion of the law.

If Jesus was capable of keeping every portion of the law, then He would be found worthy to become a sacrifice for our sin –

yours and mine. If He became a sacrifice for our sin, then all that we must do is embrace Him and His sacrificial death.

In short, then, to become saved we must:

1. Admit (we sin)
2. Repent (want to turn away from it)
3. Believe (that Jesus is the answer)
4. Embrace (the truth about Jesus)

We **admit** that we are sinner, that we have sinned. This is nothing more than agreeing with God that we have broken His law. Can you honestly say that you have not broken God's law? If we admit to breaking even the "smallest" law, then we are lawbreakers.

After we admit that we have sinned, the next step is found in **repenting**. Some believe that repenting is actually moving away from sin. This author believes that it is a willingness to move away from sin, and there is a difference.

As we have already discussed, it is impossible to stop sinning. Human beings simply cannot do it because as long as we live, we will have a sin nature, which is something within us that gives us a propensity to sin. As long as we have this inner propensity to sin or break God's laws, we will never be perfect in this life.

We cannot one day say "Lord, I promise to stop sinning." If we do that, we are only kidding ourselves and setting ourselves up for major failure. We cannot stop sinning in this life. The most we can do is *want* to stop sinning and then spend the rest of our lives allowing God to create the character of Jesus within us, slowly, little by little.

Repenting is to decide that you no longer want to do the things that keep us out of heaven. We no longer wish to break God's laws. It is not promising God that we will never sin again.

Once we admit, then repent, we must **believe**. This is one of the most difficult things to do because believing that Jesus died in our place, that He lived a perfectly sinless life, is extremely difficult to believe. Our minds cannot grasp that truth. We must ask God to open our eyes to that truth so that we can embrace it.

While on the cross next to Jesus, the one thief joined the other thief in ridiculing Jesus. Then, all of a sudden – as we read in Luke 23 – this same thief that had just been ridiculing Him now turned to Him with a new understanding.

It was this new understanding that prompted the thief to say to Jesus, *"Lord, remember me when you come into your Kingdom."* Jesus looked at the man and responded to him, *"Today, you will be with me in paradise."*

What had occurred in the mind and heart of that thief from one moment to the next? One thing, and that one thing was that God opened the thief's eyes so that he could see the truth. It was as if the blinders fell off and he now saw and understood who Jesus was, even to the most cursory degree that Jesus was dying not for Himself, but for others.

It was this understanding, this awareness that prompted the man to ask Jesus to simply be remembered. Jesus went way beyond it to promise the man that he would be with Jesus that day in paradise.

Please notice in Luke 23 that there is nothing in the chapter that tells us that the man promised Jesus he would give up sin, or that he would never sin again. There is nothing that tells us that thief took the time to enter into a final deathbed confession of his sins so that he could be absolved.

The thief made no promises to Jesus at all. What he experienced was the truth of who Jesus was and what Jesus accomplished for humanity. Jesus accomplished what we cannot. What is left is for each person to *admit, repent, believe,* and *embrace.*

Let me clarify here that though we do not see any verbal repentance from the thief, we know that he did repent. He admitted as well. How can we know this? Because of the thief's complete about-face with respect to his attitude toward Jesus. One minute he was ridiculing Jesus and the next, embracing Him. This is important. There is no way he could have or would have *embraced* Jesus had he not been humbled by the truth *about* Jesus.

Once the thief saw the truth, he was instantly humbled. Within himself, he knew that he was a sinner, and in fact the text states that this is what he told the other thief dying next to him. *"But the other answering rebuked him, saying, Dost not thou fear God, seeing thou art in the same condemnation? And we indeed justly; for we receive the due reward of our deeds: but this man hath done nothing amiss"* (Luke 23:40-41). Something happened within the heart of the one thief. In one moment, the thief went from harassing Jesus to recognizing his own sinfulness and then ultimately asking for grace, which was freely given to him.

Whether he said it or not, the thief went from haughtiness to humility in a very short space of time and it was all because he saw the truth about Jesus. That truth helped him realize that he deserved his death and what would happen to him after death. He understood that Jesus did not deserve death.

From here, the thief fully embraced the truth about Jesus and was rewarded with eternal life because of it. He did not come off the cross to be water baptized. He did not list a long litany of offenses against God. He recognized the truth about Jesus, was humbled, and embraced that truth!

This is what each of us needs to do. We cannot give in to the lie that tells us that we are not good enough, or we have not given up enough before God will accept us. We must reject the lie that says we must somehow earn our salvation.

Jesus has done everything that is necessary to make salvation available to us. The only thing that is left for us is to see the truth. Once we see that truth, it should humble us to the point of embracing Jesus and all that He stands for and is to us.

The eighth chapter of Romans begins with the fact that all who trust Jesus for salvation are no longer condemned...*ever*. All of my sins – past, present, and future – have not only been forgiven, but canceled. It is because of my faith in the atonement (death) of Jesus that God is able to cancel all of my sins, even the ones that I have not committed yet. This does not make me eager to commit them. It makes me want to do what I can to avoid sinning.

If you do not know Jesus, please do not put down this book without deliberately *believing* that He is God, that He died for you by the shedding of His blood on the cross, and that He rose three days later because death could not keep Him. Do you believe that? If you do not yet believe it, do you *want* to believe it? If so, then simply ask God to help you come to believe all that Jesus is and all that He has accomplished for you. God will answer your prayers and you may either receive instantaneous awareness of all that Jesus is and has done, or it may be a *growing* awareness over time. In either case, it is the most important decision you will ever make.

Turn to Him now and pray for knowledge of the truth and an ability to embrace it. Please. He is waiting for you.

Ask Yourself:

1. Do you *know* Jesus? Are you in *relationship* with Him? Have you had a spiritual transaction according to John 3?

2. Do you *want* to receive eternal life through the only salvation that is available?
3. Do you believe that Jesus is God the Son, who was born of a virgin, lived a sinless life, died a bloody and gruesome death to pay for your sin, was buried, and rose again on the third day? Do you *believe* this?
4. Do you *want* to *embrace* the truth from #3?
5. Pray that God will open your eyes and provide you with the faith to begin believing the truth about Jesus. Ask Him to help your faith embrace the truth, realizing that you are not good enough to save yourself and that your sin will keep you out of God's Kingdom without His salvation.
6. Pray as if your life depended upon it because *it does*!

If you have prayed to receive Jesus as Savior and Lord, please write to me. I want to send you some materials at *no charge or obligation*. Write to me at **fred_deruvo@hotmail.com** and sign up for our free bimonthly newsletter at **www.studygrowknow.com**

EPILOGUE

February 16, 2011: It is way too late. We cannot go back. Society has changed and it has changed for the worse. Unfortunately, even society has not yet seen or experienced the worst, which is yet to come.

We can write and read a multitude of books on the subject of *evil*; evil that is perpetrated from one person to another, and evil that is perpetrated on society as a whole. We can take the time to delve into the very real effects of satanic crime that occurs too often in society. What is common to most of it is the reluctance of the media to report any known satanic connection with crimes that are truly satanic in origin.

It does not matter whether we are discussing Richard Ramirez (Night Stalker), many of the Death Metal Satanic rock bands, smaller covens and groups of Satanists who have wandered stoically into the forbidden areas of Satanism and witchcraft (Wicca), people who have been famous for beginning satanic societies, individuals like David Berkowitz (Son of Sam), Charles Manson, or any number of others whose crimes have rocked urban areas – one thing stands out. This world is becoming far more *wicked*. It is almost as if the dam itself that once kept this type of evil out of the mainstream of society has nearly crumbled completely away with very little left to hold back the chaos. With but one final shove, what remains of this dam will be forced out of the way, and the emissaries of hell will vomit onto the land without restraint.

There is nothing that can be done to turn back the tide. Too much has been released into this world by invitation of a multitude of humans. A growing number of people who have wittingly or unwittingly succumbed to the temptations of the Dark Lord have invited him into their world and ultimately our world, allowing him to release his potent venom on unsuspecting masses of people.

Very few people connect the dots. Fewer still see the reality that the world of Satan is on the verge of breaking through to the world of men in all its ferocious, unchecked malevolence. I have read the Bible, and the parts that draw our attention to the end-of-the-world scenarios that are slated to occur at the end of the age are clear.

Jesus warns us in the Olivet Discourse, found in Matthew 24, Mark 13, and Luke 21. John warns us in the book of Revelation. Paul warns us in numerous epistles, as does Peter, all from the New Testament. Daniel, Isaiah, Jeremiah, Joel, and many other books or parts of books from the Old Testament seek our attention by providing details that are too *specific* too ignore.

The counsel from Scripture is very clear and very *dire*. It is absolutely impossible to turn back the hands of time. It is equally impossible to shove the things that have fallen out of Pandora's Box back into it. It simply cannot be done. What has littered society is not like so much trash that fell out of the garbage can waiting simply to be picked up and tossed out again.

The evil that has infiltrated society includes things that have moved stealthily into that society over an extended period of time. It is only when we stop to consider what life was like twenty, thirty, forty years ago or longer that we begin to understand the ramifications of what has transpired within the world since that time.

Little by little, the door has been forced open just that much more. What started out with the Beatle's fairly innocuous songs like *I Want to Hold Your Hand* have segued into more notorious tunes like Van Halen's *Running with the Devil* and the Rolling Stones' *Sympathy for the Devil.* Groups like Slayer, Satanic Black Metal, Acheron, Angel Corpse, Cradle of Filth, Blasphemy, Beherit (means "Satan" in Syriac), Burzum, and a slew of other metal bands all have anti-Christian themes in their lyrics. A number of bands have actually come out and stated that they hope their songs create an uprising *against* Christianity. What began innocently enough as a parlor game called "Ouija Board" has become a fascination with the occult and all things macabre.

Whether it has been film, books, or music, Satan has worked to worm his way into society from point A to point Z. He has seemingly left no stone unturned in his drive to become the actual god of this world's inhabitants.

The more Satan can force people to open themselves up to him, the more he is able to influence society. The more people he can entice into overtly *rejecting* God, the more those people will either begin to view themselves as deities, or they will view him as deity. When this happens, the window from his dimension to ours opens up that much wider. It seems to me that there is very little that separates our dimension from Satan's any longer. Satan couldn't care less what we worship, as long as it is not the Only Wise God. Above all things, he wants to keep that from happening. If someone loves cars, or money, or leisure time, or books, or movies, or celebrities, or travel, or whatever it happens to be, he is pleased because our eyes and interests are on ourselves.

William Kennedy has written a number of books that probe deeply into the hidden underbelly of society, the part of society that no one really wants to admit exists at all. He has connected the dots and shown that many of the events that have been reported to us in the media stem from something that is normally kept hidden from the public. No one wants to talk about satanic crime. It's too weird. It means that if Satan exists, so does God. If God exists, then what do agnostics and/or atheists do? What does *society* do?

The media does not like to delve into the supernaturally macabre. It is out of their league, and since it involves the supernatural it becomes the equivalent of the *superstitious* to most people. Since the supernatural is not provable, then why deal with it? Why mention it? Why report on it?

The answer to that is that if the perpetrators of various crimes *believe* in Satan, or some entity or form of malevolence that they worship and want to please and emulate, then it is obviously that belief system that motivates them to do the crimes they commit. If that is real to *them*, the media should not look the other way and ignore that fact. It should not matter that members of the media do not believe it, or they may think they will appear as loons. They are there to report the news. Unfortunately, in today's world the media often picks and chooses what it will report and how it will report it.

So for instance, with respect to Richard Ramirez, who was portrayed in the media as a Satanist *wannabe*, merely a dabbler in the mysticism of the occult, the point was completely missed. His actual involvement in the occult was fairly deep and it was directly due to that involvement that he committed the crimes he committed with the horror, ferocity, and pleasure that went along with them. Crime scene photos show the results of a madman, a lunatic with a bloodlust that seemed unquenchable. What he did, he did *for* Satan. What he believed burst out of the inner psychoses he experienced deep within his conflicted mind because of his love for the master he served.

If we consider how Satan – under God's watchful eye – has spent generations directing people into the hidden knowledge regarding Satanism, and through them brought the world that much closer to apocalyptic status, it becomes easy to understand how Satan has worked throughout history. In recent times – within the past one hundred or so years – people like Helena Blavatsky introduced the set of core beliefs of Satanism that has transmuted itself into what has simply become known as the New Age Movement. Through Blavatsky, a veritable smorgasbord of dark knowledge filling numerous volumes taught human beings the secrets of the universe. In many ways, this was the start of Satanism in modern times.

Others carried the torch after her, such as Annie Besant, Aleister Crowley (who referred to himself as the Beast and the Antichrist as well as Jesus Christ on various occasions), Anton LaVey (who formed the Church of Satan), Michael Aquino (who formed the Temple of Set after branching off from the Church of Satan) and many others who had either bit parts or major.

There have been many celebrities and people of renown who have ventured into the area of the dark arts. Whether as an escape from the boredom of the daily grind or to direct their lives to heights of greater knowledge through the use of *magick* is debatable, but at least some entered into agreements with the enemy of our souls.

We can go all the way back to the first century of the church only to realize that Gnosticism is a form of *Satanism* or New Ageism in that it seeks to delve into the areas of secret or hidden knowledge (gnosis). It is clear from a number of Paul's writings alone that he fought against the heresies contained within the teachings of Gnosticism.

Besides Satanism, there is also *Luciferianism*, which means instead of glorifying Satan and all that he is, specific characteristics and qualities are venerated by individuals who seek to gain them for themselves or to increase the level that may already exist within.

In each attempt to indoctrinate new people in new generations, Satan succeeds in bringing his purposes to an ever-increasing audience seemingly hungry for secret knowledge while avoiding the One God who is the only Wise God. All other gods are imposters and will never ascend to His throne.

In truth, of course, Satan is *the* imposter that presents himself in whatever guise he needs to for each individual to succumb to the temptation of knowledge and power. There is only one lesser god, who in reality is no god at all. This truth escapes those who are unable to see that God is God and there is none before Him.

Evil in this world has progressively excelled to a point of no return. What we will see from now forward is a continuing greater degree of evil until, like the days of Noah, all that exists on the earth will be the fact *"that every imagination of the thoughts of [man's] heart [will be] only evil continually"* (Genesis 6:5).

Regarding the Columbine massacre, the world was not really told about the fact that both shooters were deeply involved in Satanism on their own. In fact, the group they hung out with was dedicated to Satan. Whether it was through Black Death Metal music or whether they were simply discussing ways to worship their Dark Lord, their reality is that like all Satanists, they wanted to *inverse* the Christian order and lift up Satan to what they believed was his rightful position, while dethroning God. Because of this, the Aryan philosophy adopted by Hitler was something they themselves adopted. African Americans were considered unequal as were Christians. In fact, by killing Christians, they believed they were doing something that would bring them honor through having pleased Satan. This sounds a bit like *Islam*, doesn't it? In that ideology, it is not only permissible but radical Islamists are encouraged to kill those outside of Islam (called *infidels*), and in so doing, that individual receives honor because Allah has apparently been pleased.

It was to that end that Eric Harris and Dylan Klebold chose people to kill whose deaths would please their master. Christians were ordered to say that the shooter was their god. When they refused, they were killed. Others were asked if they believed in God and when they said "no," they were spared. African Americans were not spared in the rampage.

Both of these individuals came loaded to the gills with weapons and explosives. The fact that they had been experimenting with home-made bombs and explosives for up to a year prior to the murder spree escaped the media's attention. The media were more interested in focusing on the use of guns because that is a hot button for many people. It is clear that had not Harris and Kliebold had access to guns, they would have used bombs, which would likely have killed many more people. People who *want* to kill always find a *way* to kill.

Kennedy cites many other examples of those involved in Satanism, which led them to commit the heinous crimes they eventually committed. He also discusses aspects of the Catholic Church and many of the leaders within it along with their propensity to engage in acts that are fully unbiblical and even satanic.

It is difficult for us to believe that those who are supposedly dedicated to serving us as mentors, teachers, and pastors could possibly have given themselves over to the type of evil alleged in order to perpetrate their own malevolent desires on humanity. While we do not want to believe this, it really should not shock us to realize that it may be true, if we see the Bible as truth.

For instance, when God saw that humanity only thought about evil all the time, do we really wonder why God opted to wipe out the world with a global flood? If people were *that* evil and *that* malevolent then, so that God saw no other recourse but to utterly destroy, how can we be surprised at the level of iniquity in society today and not consider the same possible result of that unchecked evil?

It is very easy to bury one's head in the sand, refusing to acknowledge anything that smacks of the supernatural. Many are doing just that today, just like they did during the times of both Noah and Lot. We do not want to give credence to the idea that there are powers from the spiritual realm that seek their will and their way and have no problem using humanity to foist those purposes on this world. We are seeing the results of it.

Because of the tumult that has energized the population of Egypt, President Mubarak has stepped down. It does *not* end there though, because as pointed out, the Muslim Brotherhood – a virulently radical Islamic group – waits in the wings to overthrow any government that comes to power that is not radically Islamic.

Protests have been occurring in other countries as well, with Iran, Lybia, Palestine, Yemen, Tunisia, and elsewhere all yearning for freedom from what they believe to be governments that have kept them in chains. Why is this happening throughout the world *now*, seemingly all of a sudden? What has been the focal point or the catalyst that has drawn people together in one massive effort to overthrow the powers that have existed for so long? The answer may be very simple and yet no doubt unbelievable to many.

Columnist Terresa Monroe-Hamilton has voiced her opinions as to what has motivated these throngs of people to topple existing governments. She writes, *"Forces that I consider to be nothing short of evil have joined in what they see as their 'chance' to bring down the West and capitalism; to replace it with their given ideology du jour... Whether it be Islamofascism, Socialism, Communism or a progressive mixture of a number of isms, they look to ring the death knell of Western society and bring it down through glorious revolution and chaos. And the international dominoes have started to fall."*[36]

This seems to be the goal, even though the public rhetoric that is shouted has to do with wanting democracy and the freedom that it provides. She continues by stating, *"The Egyptian and Tunisian revolutions did not just spontaneously erupt. No... They are well planned, drawn out, militant efforts to bring about revolutionary change on a global scale. This will be done using the Internet and the young, who*

---

[36] http://www.worldviewweekend.com/worldview-times/article.php?articleid=6905

will be manipulated into revolt, with either legitimate causes, manufactured wrongs or a combination of both."[37]

If what Monroe-Hamilton says is true, then without doubt we have the makings of a worldwide coup that has as its goal nothing less than world *domination*. The strange part of all this is that these theories or ideas put forth by Monroe-Hamilton and others will likely come across as those espoused by the people wearing "tin hats," or the conspiracy nutcases. Who wants to be branded a conspiracy nut? It is easy to laugh these people off and disregard what they say because of the fact that their beliefs seem so preposterous.

Monroe-Hamilton tells us that she believes we may well be on the verge of seeing the last vestiges of capitalism, and with it, democracy. If that is true, then obviously something must *replace* it. If a global elite *does* exist, desiring above all things to bring their rule over the earth so that things can be done *their* way, it seems clear that the best way to accomplish this is through the ushering in of a seemingly uncontrolled chaos on a global level.

Monroe-Hamilton's opinion highlights this fact. *"Beginning to see the scope here? Americans have been out-foxed by their government who all along has been pulling together the makings of a movement that would start revolts in the Middle East and move throughout Europe and then strike at home, culminating in a New World Order. Call me crazy, but it is as clear as anything I have ever seen. While we have been working and taking care of our families, our politicians have been planning for our glorious future of bowing down before our elitist overlords. What is the end game? Well, if I had to wager, worldwide chaos and when it all falls down, a chosen few will be there to pick up the pieces of wealth and power to shape an uber-form of Communism that*

---

[37] http://www.worldviewweekend.com/worldview-times/article.php?articleid=6905

will be attempted worldwide. Conspiracy theory you say? I call it a very well-planned international coup."[38]

What we may very well be seeing is the start of the worldwide revolution that will bring utter and absolute collapse to the world's economy. It will *seem* as though it came about as an unplanned and uncontrolled event, but the fact remains that the cause of it may have been carefully planned, monitored, and manipulated until the desired result was evidenced. This truly could not have happened at any other time in history prior to today because technology has only now gotten to a point where global communication is nearly instantaneous.

Something is happening, and lest we think it is beyond the scope of God's ability to contain, we need to think again. What will undoubtedly appear to be catastrophic happenstance from our perspective is the result of God's sovereignty and will.

The individuals who have literally partnered with the devil to bring these events to pass bear the full responsibility of their actions. Just as Judas was deemed responsible for his actions in spite of the fact that Scripture foresaw it, the players in this scenario will also face judgment for their part in bringing down the established order so that Satan can bring forth his son of hell to try to bring about God's destruction.

This is exactly the ultimate goal of all of Satan's efforts now. He has had to work diligently and consistently, revealing a bit here and a bit more there until he reaches that point when his son – the Antichrist – will be revealed.

It seems as though we are very close to that happening. If the world's global economy fails, the entire system will collapse. Far from being a problem to the global elite, this will be their intended

---

[38] http://www.worldviewweekend.com/worldview-times/article.php?articleid=6905

desire. They will easily replace the former economy with one that is global in nature. They will become the gods of this age, in control of all they survey.

The economic collapse may well bring about a new world order, just as George Soros and others have been wishing for and working toward. However, their euphoria may be short-lived once they reach that state of nirvana. While the average, common person is the enemy of their goals *now*, once they have achieved their goals, *they* will become their own worst enemy and the infighting will begin. They will know what they were capable of accomplishing and begin to see one another as the enemy they need to watch.

One person will strive for one thing, while another strives for something else. Mistrust will come galloping in the door, pitting members of the global elite against one another.

The prophet Daniel teaches us that after the world becomes *one,* it is not long before that same world will be divided up into ten parts. It makes sense, because there will be too many cooks in the kitchen to allow only one individual to have voice.

To avoid problems, or possibly to curtail them, a ten-nation federacy will be created in which one individual (or possibly a small group of individuals) will rule each area of the world. Daniel 7 explains the rising and falling of four kingdoms. The fourth beast (kingdom) has ten horns and was different in nature from the previous three. Verse 8 tells us "*I considered the horns, and, behold, there came up among them another little horn, before whom there were three of the first horns plucked up by the roots: and, behold, in this horn were eyes like the eyes of man, and a mouth speaking great things."*

So we have ten horns and out of those ten horns rose another horn, which became the eleventh horn. It seems clear that this eleventh horn "plucks up" or kills three horns. So, in reality, we have a situation where ten rulers rule over the various parts of the earth after it has collapsed and congealed into one. From that oneness, the world is broken up into ten parts. It is at this point that the Antichrist (the eleventh horn) rises to his place of rule after successfully eliminating three of the ten rulers.

Once this occurs, the remaining seven rulers, as well as the rest of the global elite, fall into place and recognize Antichrist as supreme. It is from this point on that Antichrist takes his biblically prophesied place in future history as final world dictator and enters into a covenant with Israel which begins the Tribulation, lasting seven years, and which is really the beginning of the end.

Back to present day. People who believe they are agnostic or even atheistic in essence have only rejected the Living and True God, but they still have a god or gods in His rightful place in their lives. Those gods are the windows through which Satan and his hordes gain access to those individual lives and society as a whole. The more people he has to work through, the greater the damage he can inflict on society. The greater the damage, the quicker he can turn society to his purposes.

Things are without doubt ramping up to an unbelievable evil crescendo. It really should not take us by surprise, though the magnitude of it may be something that was not expected.

It is absolutely unfeasible to go backwards in time to reconstruct the same situations with different outcomes. There is currently so much evil in the world, it is as if it only waits for the signal for all of it to come out of its various hiding places in order to overthrow what remains of the good.

This evil cannot be fought against. It cannot be withstood. It cannot be hoped or even prayed away. It is here and it waits with all of its impatient malevolence. There is nothing that can be done to save society. Nothing.

What must happen now is for the invisible Church that began on the Day of Pentecost, as recorded in Acts 2, to stand up and righteously proclaim that Jesus is God and that His life, death, and resurrection paid the price as the perfect and eternal atonement for sin. Authentic Christians everywhere must be about the Master's business, and that business entails setting the captive free by instructing them in the truth. There is only one truth and it is found in Jesus alone.

We cannot save this world. We cannot even save our own society. We must acknowledge that God is true and every man a liar. God has directed the affairs of men since the beginning. He is no less in control now.

In spite of the fact that Satan and his countless horde of demonic minions are even now striving to overtake and overthrow this world, the Bible tells us that Satan's reign will be short-lived. However, during his brief stint as world ruler during the coming Tribulation, through the empowering of his diabolical incarnate son, the Antichrist, the havoc he will be allowed to wreak will make World War II seem like a thrill ride in an amusement park.

The Christian's job today is the same as it has always been. However, the times are far more dangerous and the day is almost night. We must present the gospel of Jesus Christ to anyone and everyone whether they listen or not. We must pray that they will listen and that God will open their blind eyes.

We cannot save the physical world. This we are not called to do. What we are called to do is to make disciples of people from all nations. The Great Commission is our task at hand and it must remain our task until He takes us from this world to the next.

May our Lord give us the grace, the insight, the wisdom, the gentleness, and the fervency to witness to all people that at the Name of Jesus Christ, all will willingly bow, that He might be honored.

A commentary on the book of Revelation, chapters 5 - 22, in plain English and written for the average individual. Author Fred DeRuvo draws back the curtain on chapters five through twenty-two, presenting information in an easy-to-understand style. One thing is certain regarding the book of Revelation. Because of its prophetic nature, Christians will continue to debate aspects of it until we can know for certain. Probably the most often-missed point of Revelation is the fact that it reveals the Lamb of God for who He is; King of Kings and Lord of Lords! ($17.50; 390 pages, ISBN: 978-0977424498)

We hear all the time how bad things are getting throughout the world. Do we chalk it all up to being the normal cycles that occur in life, or is something else going on behind the scenes? What if this generation alive now turns out to be the last one before Jesus returns? Is there any truth at all to the claim that Jesus will return one day? If you are one who has not taken the time to read through some of the books of the Bible that are said to teach truths regarding the last days, *Living in the Last Generation* puts it out there in a straightforward manner, making it easy to understand. ($11.95; 132 pages, ISBN: 978-0977424405)

READY FOR THE COMING SHORTAGE?

- Food and gas prices rising at astronomical rates.
- Crop failures due to extreme and unusual weather
- Limited food supplies

Yet, you have to eat. You need to feed your family. What choices do you have? You can start building up a bulk supply of foodstuffs, but how best to start and what companies can you trust?

Shelf Reliance is a company that began with people like you. They saw the need for quality bulk food, at reasonable prices and Thrive Shelf Reliance was born. Shelf Reliance foods are produced under strict standards that take potential food allergies into consideration. The foods are freeze-dried, making them long-lasting and they taste great!

Many recipes are provided by the company, with short videos showing you how to cook meals using Shelf Reliance products.

You can put your head in the sand, believing that things will all work out in the end, or you can be proactive and take steps to ensure that your family will be provided for when things get really tough. No one expected the Great Depression either. If you're unsure, purchase a sample or two of their chicken or ground beef. We're confident you will want more. Do what you can today, to provide for your family tomorrow.

For more information, visit
http://studygrowknow.shelfreliance.com

Listen to our radio program, **Study-Grow-Know,** on the following stations:

- **AM950 KAHI** or listen on their Website **www.kahi.com** Saturdays at Noon
- **Live365.com** and search for Study-Grow-Know

All of our programs are archived at our own Web site **www.studygrowknow.com** on our **BLOG** page from the MENU

Made in the USA
Charleston, SC
24 October 2011